# SIDE by SIDE

## THIRD EDITION

BOOK 1

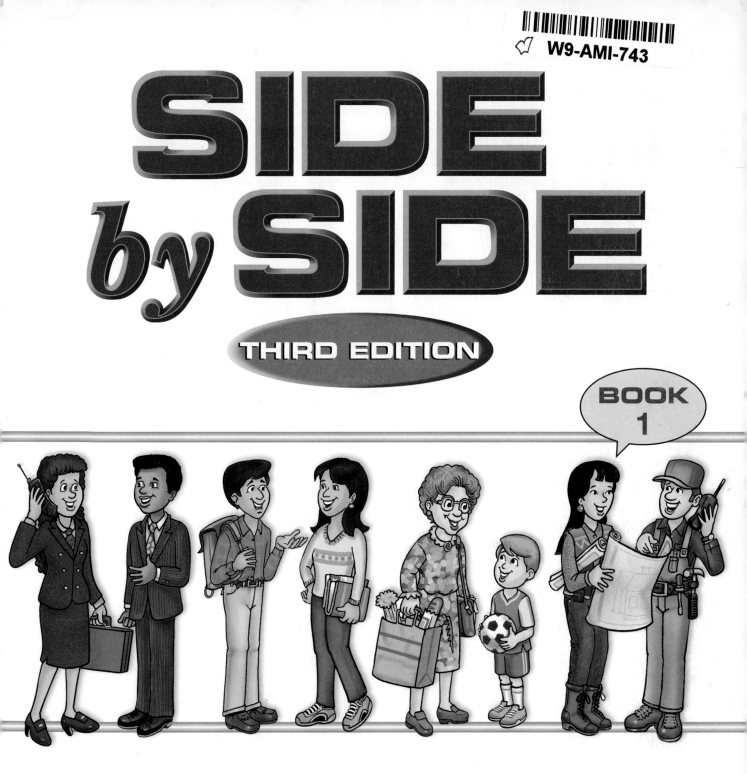

## Steven J. Molinsky
## Bill Bliss

*Illustrated by*

Richard E. Hill

Longman

# Scope and Sequence

| Chapter | Topics, Vocabulary & Math | Grammar | Functional Communication | Listening & Pronunciation | Writing |
|---|---|---|---|---|---|
| 1 | • Personal information<br>• Meeting people<br>• Alphabet<br>• Spelling names aloud<br>• Cardinal numbers in addresses and telephone numbers | • To be: Introduction | • Meeting people | • Listening for personal information<br>• Pronouncing linked sounds | • Writing about yourself: Name, address, phone number, country of origin<br>• Filling out a form<br>• Addressing an envelope |
| 2 | • Classroom objects<br>• Rooms in the home<br>• Cities & nationalities<br>• Places around town | • To be + location<br>• Subject pronouns | • Greeting people | • Listening for information about people's locations<br>• Pronouncing reduced *and* | • Making a list of classroom objects |
| 3 | • Everyday activities | • Present continuous tense | • Checking understanding | • Listening and responding correctly to questions about people's actions<br>• Pronouncing reduced *What are* & *Where are* | • Writing about your current activities and the activities of friends |
| Gazette | • Titles & nicknames<br>• Common leisure activities: playing instruments, sports, & games<br>• Culture concept: Greetings around the world<br>• Telephone numbers | • To be<br>• Present continuous tense | • Describing people's activities | • Listening to messages on a telephone answering machine | • Writing an e-mail or instant message to tell about yourself |
| 4 | • Everyday activities | • To be: Short answers<br>• Possessive adjectives | • Attracting someone's attention | • Listening & responding correctly to questions about activities<br>• Pronouncing deleted *h* | • Writing about a place in your community |
| 5 | • Describing people & things<br>• Weather<br>• Fahrenheit & Celsius temperatures | • To be: Yes/No questions, Short answers<br>• Adjectives<br>• Possessive nouns | • Calling someone you know on the telephone | • Listening & responding correctly to requests for information<br>• Pronouncing yes/no questions with *or* | • Filling out a form<br>• Writing a friendly letter describing the weather and current activities |
| 6 | • Family members<br>• Describing activities & events | • To be: Review<br>• Present continuous tense: Review<br>• Prepositions of location | • Introducing people | • Listening & making deductions<br>• Pronouncing stressed and unstressed words | • Writing a story about a scene<br>• Writing about a favorite photograph |
| Gazette | • Family relations<br>• Classroom activities<br>• Culture concept: Extended & nuclear families | • To be<br>• Possessive adjectives | • Describing family members and family relationships | • Listening to and interpreting correctly radio weather forecasts | • Writing about your family<br>• Writing an e-mail or instant message to tell about the weather and current activities |

# Lifeskills, Test Preparation, Curriculum Standards and Frameworks

| Lifeskills & Test Preparation | EFF | SCANS/Employment Competencies | CASAS | LAUSD | LCPs |
|---|---|---|---|---|---|
| • Personal information & forms<br>• Information on an envelope<br>• Common abbreviations in addresses | • Gather information<br>• Cooperate with others | • Sociability<br>• Acquire & evaluate information | 0.1.2, 0.1.4, 0.1.6, 0.2.1, 0.2.2, 2.4.1, 5.1.4 | 1, 2, 3, 4, 5, 7, 8, 11b, 41, 58, 60 | 18.06, 22.01, 22.02, 22.03, 25.01, 32.12, 33.02, 33.07 |
| • Classroom items<br>• Simple classroom commands<br>• School personnel<br>• School locations<br>• Locating classroom items | • Manage resources: Identify those resources you have; Determine where they are<br>• Work together<br>• Give direction | • Identify resources<br>• Participate as a member of a team<br>• See things in the mind's eye (Draw a picture or diagram) | 0.1.2, 0.1.4, 0.1.5 | 9a, 15, 16, 17, 18 | 22.01, 22.02, 22.03, 33.01, 33.02, 33.04, 33.07, 33.09 |
| • Common classroom & home activities<br>• Asking about home activities | • Seek input from others<br>• Identify a strong sense of family | • Identify goal-relevant activities | 0.1.4, 0.1.5, 0.1.6, 0.2.4 | 9c, 11a, 12, 13 | 22.01, 33.01, 33.02, 33.04, 33.07, 33.09 |
| • Identifying people by appropriate titles<br>• Interpreting telephone messages on an answering machine | • Respect others & value diversity<br>• Use technology & other tools to accomplish goals | • Acquire & evaluate information<br>• Work with cultural diversity<br>• Work with technology (telephone answering device) | 0.1.4, 0.2.3, 0.2.4, 2.1.7, 2.7.2, 4.5.4 | 1, 4, 9c, 12 | 22.04, 25.01, 23.02, 32.08, 33.01, 33.02 |
| • Common classroom & home activities<br>• Asking about home activities<br>• Learning skill: Alphabetizing | • Meet family needs & responsibilities<br>• Work within the big picture<br>• Observe critically | • Identify goal-relevant activities<br>• Responsibility<br>• Understand a social system (an apartment building & residents' activities) | 0.1.4, 0.2.4, 7.2.3, 7.4.5 | 9d, 12, 13, 58 | 22.03, 33.07, 33.09 |
| • Describing people, things, & weather<br>• Using the telephone<br>• Interpreting a thermometer<br>• Weather reports | • Seek input from others | • Sociability | 0.1.2, 0.2.2, 1.1.5, 2.1.8, 2.3.3 | 6, 7, 28, 29 | 22.01, 22.02, 23.02, 30.01, 32.12, 33.01, 33.03 |
| • Family relations<br>• Common activities<br>• Greeting & introducing<br>• Learning skill: Categorizing<br>• Eye contact & gestures | • Seek input from others<br>• Identify family relationships<br>• Develop & express sense of self<br>• Cooperate with others | • Sociability<br>• Self-esteem | 0.1.1, 0.1.2, 0.1.4, 0.2.1, 0.2.4, 7.2.3 | 6, 9b | 22.02, 22.03, 22.04, 31.01, 33.02, 33.09 |
| • Family relations<br>• Common classroom activities<br>• Weather forecasts | • Identify the family system<br>• Identify supportive family relationships<br>• Respect others & value diversity<br>• Use technology & other tools to accomplish goals | • See things in the mind's eye (Interpret a chart; Draw a chart)<br>• Identify goal-relevant activities<br>• Work with cultural diversity | 0.1.5, 0.2.3, 2.3.3, 2.7.2 | 6, 12, 28 | 30.01, 31.01, 32.08, 33.02 |

**EFF:** Equipped for the Future (Content standards, Common activities, & Key activities for Citizen/Community Member, Worker, & Parent/Family role maps; EFF Communication and Reflection/Evaluation skills are covered in every chapter)

**SCANS:** Secretary's Commission on Achieving Necessary Skills (U.S. Department of Labor)

**CASAS:** Comprehensive Adult Student Assessment System

**LAUSD:** Los Angeles Unified School District (ESL Beginning Low content standards)

**LCPs:** Literacy Completion Points (Florida & Texas: Level B Workforce Development Skills & Life Skills. The following LCPs are covered in every chapter: 32.01–32.05, 32.10, 32.13, 33.01, 33.02, 34.01–34.03)

# Scope and Sequence

## ALL-SKILLS COMMUNICATION: LISTENING, SPEAKING, READING, WRITING

| Chapter | Topics, Vocabulary & Math | Grammar | Functional Communication | Listening & Pronunciation | Writing |
|---|---|---|---|---|---|
| 7 | • Places around town<br>• Locating places<br>• Describing neighborhoods<br>• Describing apartments<br>• Cardinal numbers indicating quantity | • Prepositions<br>• There is /There are<br>• Singular/Plural introduction | • Expressing gratitude | • Listening for information about neighborhoods & apartments<br>• Using rising intonation to check understanding | • Writing a description of a neighborhood<br>• Writing about your apartment building or home |
| 8 | • Clothing<br>• Colors<br>• Shopping for clothing<br>• Cardinal numbers indicating coin and currency denominations, prices, & clothing sizes | • Singular/Plural<br>• Adjectives<br>• This/That/These/Those | • Complimenting | • Listening for information about clothing items<br>• Pronouncing emphasized words | • Writing a description of clothing and colors |
| Gazette | • Clothing, colors, and cultures<br>• Culture concept: People's homes around the world<br>• Civics concept: Urban, suburban, and rural communities<br>• Interpreting percents in a pie chart | • Singular/Plural<br>• Adjectives | • Describing clothing<br>• Complimenting<br>• Describing homes | • Listening for information in public address announcements in stores | • Writing an e-mail or instant message to describe your neighborhood |
| 9 | • Language & nationalities<br>• Everyday activities | • Simple present tense | • Hesitating | • Listening for –s vs. non –s endings in verbs contained in sentences<br>• Blending with does | • Writing about your city, language, and daily activities |
| 10 | • Habitual actions<br>• People's interests & activities<br>• Days of the week<br>• The calendar<br>• Language & nationalities | • Simple present tense: Yes/No questions, Negatives, Short answers | • Starting a conversation | • Listening for information about people's habitual actions<br>• Pronouncing reduced of | • Writing about usual activities during the week and on the weekend |
| Gazette | • Languages around the world<br>• Interpreting tables with number facts in millions<br>• Culture concept: Exercising around the world | • Simple present tense | • Describing everyday activities and interests | • Listening for information in a recorded telephone announcement | • Writing an e-mail or instant message to tell about activities & interests |
| 11 | • Describing frequency of actions<br>• Describing people<br>• The calendar<br>• Time expressions<br>• Interpreting percentages related to adverbs of frequency | • Object pronouns<br>• Simple present tense: –s vs. non –s endings<br>• Have/Has<br>• Adverbs of frequency | • Reacting to information | • Pronouncing past tense endings<br>• Pronouncing deleted h<br>• Listening and making deductions | • Writing about close friends<br>• Writing about daily activities |
| 12 | • Feelings & emotions<br>• Describing usual & unusual activities | • Contrast: Simple present & present continuous tenses | • Reacting to bad news | • Listening to distinguish questions about current vs. habitual actions<br>• Pronouncing reduced to | • Writing about a typical day in a city or town |

## LIFESKILLS, TEST PREPARATION, CURRICULUM STANDARDS AND FRAMEWORKS

| Lifeskills & Test Preparation | EFF | SCANS/Employment Competencies | CASAS | LAUSD | LCPs |
|---|---|---|---|---|---|
| • Identifying & locating places in the community<br>• Identifying rooms, furniture, & fixtures in a residence<br>• Inquiring about residences, rentals, & neighborhoods<br>• Interpreting a map | • Seek input from others<br>• Provide for family members' safety & physical needs<br>• Gather information | • Identify resources<br>• Acquire & evaluate information<br>• See things in the mind's eye (Interpret a map; Draw a simple map) | 0.1.2, 0.1.4, 1.1.3, 1.4.1, 1.4.2, 2.2.1, 2.5.1, 2.5.3 | 9d, 22, 23, 38, 39 | 22.03, 25.01, 28.04, 29.01, 33.04, 33.06 |
| • Clothing<br>• Asking for help<br>• Identifying clothing needs<br>• Money: Coins, Bills<br>• Clothing labels: Sizes, Prices, Colors | • Manage resources<br>• Seek & receive assistance<br>• Resolve conflict & negotiate<br>• Interact in a way that is friendly & courteous<br>• Meet family needs & responsibilities | • Identify resources<br>• Negotiate<br>• Problem solving<br>• Sociability | 0.1.4, 1.1.6, 1.1.9, 1.2.1, 1.3.9 | 9d, 30, 31, 33, 34 | 22.03, 25.01, 25.05, 28.02, 28.03, 33.03, 33.05, 33.06 |
| • Clothing<br>• Store announcements<br>• Describing housing and neighborhoods | • Respect others & value diversity<br>• Analyze & use information<br>• Understand, interpret, & work with symbolic information<br>• Use technology & other tools to accomplish goals | • Work with cultural diversity<br>• See things in the mind's eye (Interpret a pie chart)<br>• Sociability | 0.1.4, 0.2.3, 1.1.3, 1.3.7, 1.3.9, 1.4.1, 2.7.2, 6.4.2, 6.7.4, 6.8.1 | 33, 34 | 28.02, 28.04, 32.09 |
| • Asking for and giving personal information: Name, city, language, daily activities<br>• Common activities<br>• Social interactions | • Seek input from others<br>• Develop & express sense of self<br>• Promote values, ethics, & cultural heritage within the family | • Sociability<br>• Self-esteem | 0.1.4, 0.2.1, 0.2.4 | 13 | 18.02, 22.01, 33.01, 33.02, 33.07 |
| • Common activities: Daily life, sports, recreation, & entertainment<br>• Ordering in a fast food restaurant<br>• Days of the week | • Manage resources: Allocate time<br>• Offer clear input on own interests<br>• Identify a strong sense of family | • Allocate time<br>• Self-management<br>• Sociability | 0.1.2, 0.1.3, 0.1.4, 0.2.4, 2.6.4 | 12, 13, 14a, 37 | 20.02, 22.01, 25.03, 28.01, 33.01, 33.02, 33.07 |
| • Describe common activities<br>• Interpreting recorded telephone announcements | • Analyze & use information<br>• Understand, interpret, & work with numbers & symbolic information<br>• Respect others & value diversity<br>• Use technology & other tools to accomplish goals | • See things in the mind's eye (Interpret a map)<br>• Acquire & evaluate information<br>• Work with cultural diversity<br>• Work with technology (recorded telephone announcement) | 0.2.3, 1.1.3, 2.1.7, 2.6.1, 2.7.2, 6.8.1 | 12, 23 | 22.01, 23.02, 32.08 |
| • Family relations<br>• Asking for tableware<br>• Describing oneself | • Manage resources: Allocate time<br>• Develop & express sense of self<br>• Identify a strong sense of family<br>• Interact in a way that is friendly | • Allocate time<br>• Self-esteem<br>• Sociability | 0.1.2, 0.1.4, 0.2.4 | 6 | 22.01, 22.03, 25.03, 33.01, 33.07, 33.08 |
| • Describing states of being<br>• Asking about home activities | • Identify problems<br>• Work within the big picture<br>• Identify community needs & resources | • Self-management<br>• Creative thinking<br>• Understand an organizational system (workplace operations) | 0.1.4, 0.2.4, 2.2.2, 2.2.3 | 24, 60 | 22.01, 22.03, 30.01, 33.02, 33.03 |

# Scope and Sequence

| Chapter | Topics, Vocabulary & Math | Grammar | Functional Communication | Listening & Pronunciation | Writing |
|---|---|---|---|---|---|
| **Gazette** | • Traffic: A global problem<br>• Culture concept: Modes of transportation around the world<br>• Interpreting tables with number facts in millions | • Simple present tense | • Describing a problem<br>• Describing customary activities | • Listening for information in radio news reports | • Writing an e-mail or instant message to tell about yourself, family, & personal appearance |
| **13** | • Expressing ability<br>• Occupations<br>• Looking for a job<br>• Responding to questions in a simple job interview<br>• Expressing obligation<br>• Invitations<br>• Applying for a driver's license | • Can<br>• Have to | • Apologizing | • Listening for information about occupational skills<br>• Pronouncing *can* & *can't* | • Filling out a job application form<br>• Writing about how to apply for a passport, marriage license, or loan<br>• Writing about what you have to do this week |
| **14** | • Time<br>• Months of the year<br>• Seasons<br>• Describing future plans & intentions<br>• Expressing wants<br>• Weather forecasts<br>• Making predictions<br>• Ordinal numbers | • Future: Going to<br>• Time expressions<br>• Want to | • Asking the time | • Listening for time expressions<br>• Pronouncing *going to* & *want to* | • Writing about plans for tomorrow |
| **Gazette** | • Time zones<br>• Culture concept: Notions of time and punctuality in different cultures | • Verb: To be<br>• Simple present tense<br>• Future: Going to | • Describing occupation | • Listening for movie listing information in a recorded telephone announcement | • Writing an e-mail or instant message to tell about plans for the weekend |
| **15** | • Past actions & activities<br>• Ailments<br>• Describing an event<br>• Making a doctor's appointment<br>• Numbers: Interpreting a thermometer & a dosage cup | • Past tense: Regular verbs, Introduction to irregular verbs | • Saying how you feel | • Listening to distinguish statements in the present tense vs. the past tense<br>• Pronouncing past tense endings | • Writing about a party<br>• Writing about your meals yesterday |
| **16** | • Reporting past actions & activities<br>• Giving reasons<br>• Giving excuses<br>• Using clock times in a narrative | • Past tense: Yes/No questions, Short answers, WH- questions, More irregular verbs<br>• Time expressions | • Giving an excuse | • Listening for specific information to complete a checklist<br>• Pronouncing *Did you* | • Writing about your activities yesterday |
| **17** | • Television commercials<br>• Describing physical states & emotions<br>• Telling about the past<br>• Biographies & autobiographies | • To be: Past tense | • Recommending products | • Listening to distinguish present vs. past facts<br>• Using correct intonation with yes/no questions and WH- questions | • Writing a brief autobiography about major life events (born, grew up, went to school, studied, moved)<br>• Writing about your childhood (appearance, friends, activities) |
| **Gazette** | • Advertisements<br>• Opposites<br>• Culture concept: Shopping around the world | • Tense review<br>• Adjectives | • Describing products<br>• Telling about activities in the past | • Listening for information in radio advertisements | • Writing an e-mail or instant message to tell about what you did today |

# LIFESKILLS, TEST PREPARATION, CURRICULUM STANDARDS AND FRAMEWORKS

| Lifeskills & Test Preparation | EFF | SCANS/Employment Competencies | CASAS | LAUSD | LCPs |
|---|---|---|---|---|---|
| • Describing modes of travel to work and school<br>• Interpreting traffic information & other information in radio newscasts | • Identify problems & alternative solutions<br>• Respect others & value diversity<br>• Analyze & use information<br>• Understand, interpret, & work with numbers<br>• Use technology & other tools to accomplish goals | • Acquire & evaluate information<br>• Work with cultural diversity | 0.2.3, 2.2.3, 2.7.2, 6.8.1 | 13, 24 | 26.01, 32.08, 33.02 |
| • Occupations, abilities, & skills<br>• Requesting permission to leave work<br>• Calling to explain absence<br>• "Help wanted" signs<br>• Classified ads<br>• Police/safety commands & signs | • Develop & express sense of self<br>• Plan: Set a goal; Develop an organized approach of activities & objectives<br>• Define what one is trying to achieve<br>• Interact in a way that is tactful<br>• Reflect & evaluate<br>• Work within the big picture | • Identify human resources (work skills)<br>• Self-management: Assess self accurately<br>• Self-esteem<br>• Understand an organizational system (motor vehicles department) | 0.1.2, 0.1.3, 0.2.4, 1.9.1, 2.2.2, 2.5.4, 2.5.7, 3.1.1, 3.3.3, 3.4.1, 4.1.2, 4.1.3, 4.1.5, 4.1.6, 4.1.8, 4.3.1, 4.4.1 | 10, 14b, 42, 48, 49, 50, 51, 52, 53, 54, 57, 60 | 18.01, 18.02, 18.03, 18.06, 19.01, 20.02, 22.03, 26.05, 27.02 |
| • Asking & telling time<br>• Congratulating<br>• National holidays in the United States & Canada<br>• The calendar<br>• Ordinal numbers<br>• Months of the year<br>• Filling out a form | • Create & pursue vision & goals<br>• Make a prediction<br>• Identify opportunities for each family member to experience success | • Identify goal-relevant activities<br>• Self-management: Set personal goals | 0.1.1, 0.1.2, 0.2.2, 0.2.4, 2.3.1, 2.3.2, 2.3.3, 2.7.1 | 3, 7, 13, 25, 26, 40, 60 | 25.01, 25.02, 25.03, 25.04, 29.03, 30.01, 33.02, 33.08 |
| • Identifying time zones<br>• Identifying occupations<br>• Interpreting movie listings in telephone recorded announcements | • Analyze & use information<br>• Understand, interpret, & work with symbolic information<br>• Respect others & value diversity<br>• Use technology & other tools to accomplish goals | • Acquire & evaluate information<br>• Identify human resources (occupations)<br>• Work with cultural diversity<br>• Responsibility | 0.2.3, 2.1.3, 2.6.2, 2.7.2, 4.1.8 | 13, 23, 50 | 19.01, 23.02, 25.02, 30.02, 32.08 |
| • Medical care: Parts of the body<br>• Ailments<br>• Calling for medical appointments<br>• Calling for emergency assistance<br>• Over-the-counter medications<br>• Drug labels & dosages<br>• Filling/Refilling prescriptions<br>• Interpreting a Fahrenheit thermometer<br>• Interpreting a dosage cup | • Provide for safety & physical needs of family members and self<br>• Seek & receive assistance | • Self-management<br>• Responsibility | 1.3.7, 2.1.2, 2.1.8, 2.5.1, 3.1.1, 3.1.2, 3.3.1, 3.3.2 | 19, 20, 21, 32, 43, 44, 45, 60 | 22.03, 23.01, 24.01, 24.03, 24.04, 33.02 |
| • Apologizing for lateness at work<br>• Safety procedures: Earthquake, Clothing on fire<br>• Eye contact & gestures | • Manage resources: Allocate time<br>• Balance individual roles & needs with those of the organization<br>• Develop & express sense of self | • Responsibility<br>• Integrity<br>• Allocate time | 0.1.1, 0.1.6, 1.3.7, 3.4.2, 4.3.1 | 11c, 32, 47, 60 | 19.01, 22.01, 22.04, 27.01, 33.02 |
| • Basic foods & common containers<br>• System of weights using ounces & pounds<br>• Food ads<br>• Learning skill: Categorizing | • Promote family members' growth & development<br>• Develop & express sense of self<br>• Use math to solve problems | • Self-management<br>• Serve clients/customers<br>• Responsibility<br>• Self-esteem | 0.1.3, 0.2.1, 0.2.4, 1.3.8, 1.6.1 | 35, 36, 60 | 22.01, 22.03, 28.01, 28.03, 32.07, 33.02, 33.03, 33.07 |
| • Interpreting advertisements | • Analyze & use information<br>• Respect others & value diversity<br>• Use technology & other tools to accomplish goals | • Acquire & evaluate information<br>• Work with cultural diversity | 0.2.3, 1.1.7, 1.2.1, 1.2.5, 1.3.1, 2.7.2, 7.2.3 | 22, 34 | 28.03, 33.03 |

Dear Friends,

Thank you for choosing Side by Side as your English textbook!

The mission of Side by Side has always been to offer learners a dynamic and communicative approach to help them develop the language skills they need in order to use English effectively in daily life, in the community, in school, at work, and in general, to achieve their hopes and dreams.

While the curriculum comprehensively integrates lifeskills, workplace communication, and other relevant topics, Side by Side is solidly and proudly a grammar-based program that attempts to build upon our profession's most important developments in research and practice over the decades. The text's research-based grammatical sequence is rooted in the important work of linguists of the 1940s and 1950s. Its instructional methodology reflects the exciting innovations in communicative language teaching that emerged in the 1960s and 1970s. And the 21st-century relevance of its lifeskill topics is based on the past three decades of development of competency-based approaches to language instruction, including current national, state, and local standards-based curricula you can find in the Scope & Sequence on the previous pages.

The core methodology of Side by Side's communicative approach is the guided conversation – the brief dialog that engages students in meaningful conversational exchanges within carefully structured frameworks, and then encourages students to break away from the text and use these frameworks to create conversations on their own. This practice becomes the context and springboard for the reading, writing, listening, pronunciation, role-playing, and discussion activities that follow.

Our objective is to help you create a classroom environment in which students dynamically interact with each other – working together to develop their language skills "side by side." We also believe that language instruction is most powerful when it is joyful. There is magic in the power of humor, fun, games, and music to encourage students to take risks with their emerging language, to "play" with it, and to allow their personalities to shine through as their language skills increase.

As a new generation of language learners now uses this program, we believe more strongly than ever that as we meet the demands to fill our lesson plans with competencies and content, we must also take care to preserve our role as true teachers of language – helping students develop the competence and confidence to use English creatively to meet their own needs, life circumstances, and goals – today and in the future.

We are deeply honored by your support over the years, and we promise to continue working hard to help you provide students with a language learning experience that is dynamic . . . interactive . . . and fun!

**Steven J. Molinsky**
**Bill Bliss**

# SIDE by SIDE

## THIRD EDITION

### BOOK 1

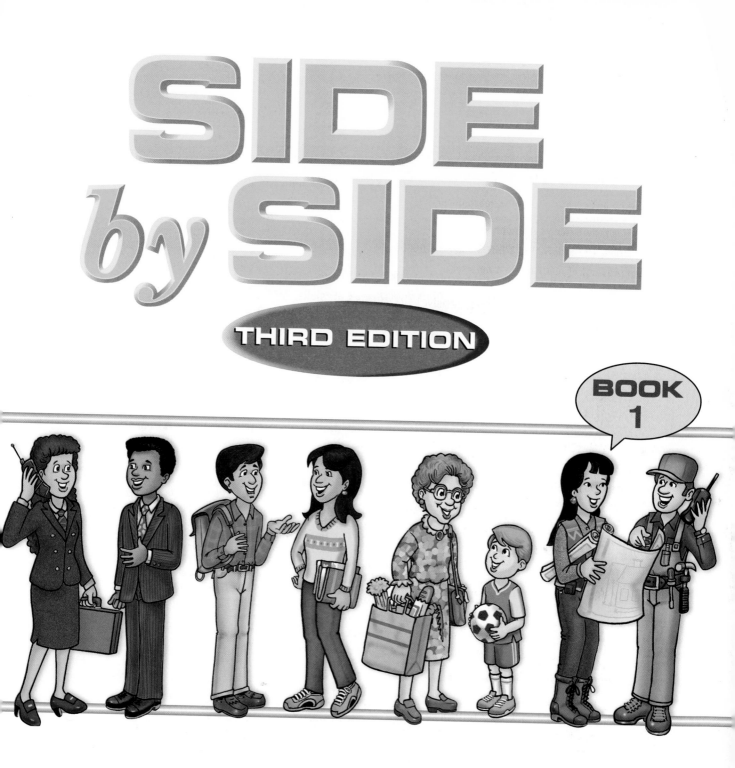

# Steven J. Molinsky
# Bill Bliss

*Illustrated by*

Richard E. Hill

**Side by Side, 3rd edition**
**Student Book 1**

Pearson Education, 10 Bank Street, White Plains, NY 10606

Vice president, director of publishing: *Allen Ascher*
Editorial manager: *Pam Fishman*
Vice president, director of design and production: *Rhea Banker*
Associate director of electronic production: *Aliza Greenblatt*
Production manager: *Ray Keating*
Director of manufacturing: *Patrice Fraccio*
Digital layout specialist: *Wendy Wolf*
Associate art director: *Elizabeth Carlson*
Interior design: *Elizabeth Carlson, Wendy Wolf*
Cover design: *Elizabeth Carlson*

Contributing *Side by Side* Gazette authors: *Laura English, Meredith Westfall*

Photo credits: p. 25, Walter Hodges/Corbis; p. 26, (*top, left*) Rhoda Sidney/Stock Boston, (*top, right*) Stuart Cohen/The Image Works, (*bottom, left*) Will & Deni McIntyre/Tony Stone Images, NY, (*bottom, right*) Ariel Skelley/The Stock Market; p. 54, (*top*) Spencer Grant/Liaison Agency, Inc., (*bottom*) Bachmann/The Image Works; p. 77, (*center*) Liane Enkelis/Stock Boston, (*left*) Bill Horsman/Stock Boston, (*right*) Robert Nickelsberg/Liaison Agency, Inc.; p. 78, (*top*) John Coletti/Stock Boston, (*second from top*) Torleif Svensson/The Stock Market, (*second from bottom*) Rick Smolan/Stock Boston, (*bottom*) Monika Graff/Stock Boston; p. 98 (*top*) Randi Anglin/The Image Works, (*second from top*) David S. Robbins/Tony Stone Images, NY, (*second from bottom*) Richemond/The Image Works, (*bottom*) Tony Stone Images, NY; p. 115, Starr/Stock Boston; p. 116, (*top left*) Topham/The Image Works, (*botom, left*) Paolo Negri/Tony Stone Images, NY, (*center*) G. Salomone, Granata Press/The Image Works, (*right*) T & D McCarthy/The Stock Market; p. 140, (*top*) John Coletti/Stock Boston, (*center*) Index Stock Photography, (*bottom*) David Simson/Stock Boston; p. 165, (*bottom, right*) Eric Sander/Liaison Agency, Inc., (*top*) Jeff Greenberg/The Image Works, (*bottom, left*) Lee Snider/The Image Works; p. 166, (*top, left*) Jeff Greenberg/The Image Works, (*top, center*) Owen Franken/Corbis, (*top, right*) David Young-Wolff/Tony Stone Images, NY, (*bottom, left*) Frank Siteman/Omni-Photo Communications, Inc., (*bottom, center*) Willie L. Hill/The Image Works, (*bottom, right*) David Young-Wolff/PhotoEdit.

The authors gratefully acknowledge the contribution of Tina Carver in the development of the original *Side by Side* program.

**Library of Congress Cataloging-in-Publication Data**

Molinsky, Steven J.
    Side by side / Steven J. Molinsky, Bill Bliss,
      p. cm.

      1. English language—Conversation and phrase books.  2. English
    language—Textbooks for foreign speakers.  I. Bliss, Bill.  II. Title.

PE1131.M576 2000
428.3'4—dc21
                      00-044990

ISBN 0-13-026744-9   (Regular Edition)

21 22 23 –V082 –13 12 11 10 09

ISBN 0-13-111959-1   (Regular Edition with Audio Highlights)

14 15 16 17 –V082 –13 12 11 10 09

ISBN 0-13-183934-9   (International Edition)

15 16 17 –V082 –13 12 11 10 09

Printed in the United States of America

# CONTENTS

# 1

## To Be: Introduction

- **Personal Information**
- **Meeting People**

### VOCABULARY PREVIEW

**①**
| | | | | | | |
|---|---|---|---|---|---|---|
| Aa | Bb | Cc | Dd | Ee | Ff | Gg |
| Hh | Ii | Jj | Kk | Ll | Mm | Nn |
| Oo | Pp | Qq | Rr | Ss | Tt | Uu |
| Vv | Ww | Xx | Yy | Zz | | |

**②** 0   1   2   3   4   5   6   7   8   9   10

**1.** alphabet      **2.** numbers

**3.** name

**4.** address

**5.** telephone number
phone number

# What's Your Name?

On the chalkboard:
- What's* your name?
- What's your address?
- What's your phone number?
- Where are you from?

In the speech bubble:
- My name is Maria.
- My address is 235* Main Street.
- My phone number is 741-8906.*
- I'm from Mexico City.

\* What's = What is
235 = two thirty-five
741-8906 = seven four one – eight nine "oh" six

## Answer these questions.

**1.** What's your name?

My name is Lorena.

**2.** What's your address?

My address is 6042 s 75 ct.

**3.** What's your phone number?

My phone number is (708) 594-67-30

**4.** Where are you from?

I'm from MEXiCO.

**Now practice with other students in your class.**

## ROLE PLAY   *A Famous Person*

Interview a famous person.  Make up addresses, phone numbers, and cities.  Use your imagination!  Practice with another student.  Then present your role play to the class.

**A.** What's your name?

**B.** My name is _Lorena Ochoa_.

**A.** _____ address?

**B.** _____.

**A.** _____ phone number?

**B.** _____.

**A.** Where are you from?

**B.** _____.

*a famous actor*

*a famous actress*

*a famous athlete*

*the president\**
*of your country*

## How to Say It!

**Meeting People**

**A.** Hello.  My name is *Peter Lewis.*
**B.** Hi.  I'm *Nancy Lee.*  Nice to meet you.
**A.** Nice to meet you, too.

**Practice conversations with other students.**

\* president / prime minister / leader

## WHAT'S YOUR NAME?

My name is David Carter. I'm American. I'm from San Francisco.

My name is Mrs. Grant. My phone number is 549-2376.

My name is Ms. Martinez. My telephone number is (213) 694-5555. My fax number is (213) 694-5557.

My name is Peter Black. My address is 378 Main Street, Waterville, Florida. My license number is 921DCG.

My name is Susan Miller. My apartment number is 4-B.

My name is Mr. Santini. My e-mail address is TeacherJoe@worldnet.com.*

My name is William Chen. My address is 294 River Street, Brooklyn, New York. My telephone number is 469-7750. My social security number is 044-35-9862.

* "TeacherJoe at worldnet-dot-com"

# ✔ READING *CHECK-UP*

## MATCH

_d_ **1.** name
_e_ **2.** address
_a_ **3.** phone number
_b_ **4.** apartment number
_f_ **5.** social security number
_c_ **6.** e-mail address

a. 549-2376
b. 4-B
c. TeacherJoe@worldnet.com
d. William Chen
e. 378 Main Street
f. 044-35-9862

## LISTENING

**Listen and choose the correct answer.**

**1.** a. Mary Black
　　b. Mrs. Grant

**2.** a. 265 River Street
　　b. 265 Main Street

**3.** a. 5-C
　　b. 9-D

**4.** a. 295-4870
　　b. 259-4087

**5.** a. 032-98-6175
　　b. 032-89-6179

**6.** a. maryb@worldnet.com
　　b. garyd@worldnet.com

## INTERVIEW *Spelling Names*

**Practice the conversation.**

**A.** What's your last name?
**B.** *Kelly.*
**A.** How do you spell that?
**B.** *K-E-L-L-Y.*
**A.** What's your first name?
**B.** *Sarah.*
**A.** How do you spell that?
**B.** *S-A-R-A-H.*

**Now interview students in your class.**

| | LAST NAME | FIRST NAME |
|---|---|---|
| **1.** | | |
| **2.** | | |
| **3.** | | |
| **4.** | | |
| **5.** | | |
| **6.** | | |
| **7.** | | |
| **8.** | | |

**Listen. Then say it.**

My name is Maria.

My address is 10 Main Street.

My apartment number is 3B.

**Say it. Then listen.**

My name is David.

My address is 9 River Street.

My phone number is 941-2238.

**SIDE by SIDE JOURNAL**

**Write about yourself in your journal.**

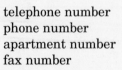

My name is _____ .

My address is _____ .

My phone number is _____ .

I'm from _____ .

# CHAPTER SUMMARY

## GRAMMAR

### To Be

| am | I am from Mexico City. (I am) |
|---|---|
| is | What's your name? (What is) My name is Maria. |
| are | Where are you from? |

## KEY VOCABULARY

### Personal Information

name
first name
last name
address
e-mail address

telephone number
phone number
apartment number
fax number

### Meeting People

Hello.
Hi.

My name is _____.
I'm _____.

Nice to meet you.
  Nice to meet you, too.

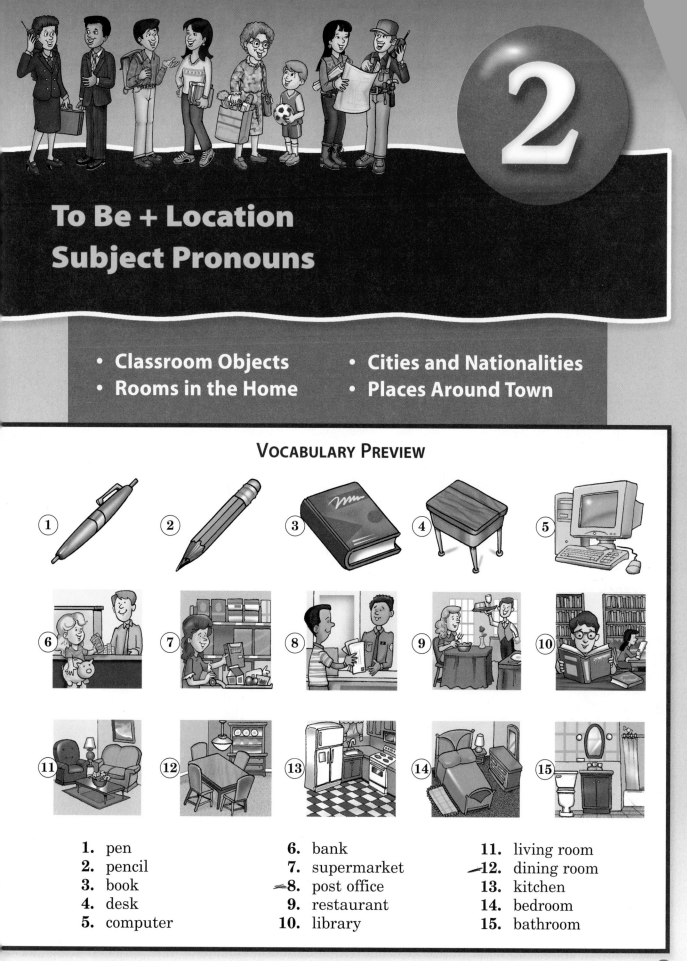

# 2

## To Be + Location
## Subject Pronouns

- **Classroom Objects**
- **Rooms in the Home**
- **Cities and Nationalities**
- **Places Around Town**

### VOCABULARY PREVIEW

1. pen
2. pencil
3. book
4. desk
5. computer
6. bank
7. supermarket
8. post office
9. restaurant
10. library
11. living room
12. dining room
13. kitchen
14. bedroom
15. bathroom

| | | | |
|---|---|---|---|
| **1.** pen | **6.** globe | **10.** clock | **14.** chair |
| **2.** book | **7.** map | **11.** bulletin board | **15.** ruler |
| **3.** pencil | **8.** board | **12.** computer | **16.** desk |
| **4.** notebook | **9.** wall | **13.** table | **17.** dictionary |
| **5.** bookshelf | | | |

# Where Is It?

# At Home

1. living room
2. dining room
3. kitchen
4. bedroom
5. bathroom
6. attic
7. yard
8. garage
9. basement

# Where Are You?

| Where | am | I | ? |
|-------|-----|------------------|---|
|       | is  | { he / she / it }|   |
|       | are | { we / you / they }| |

| (I am) | I'm | |
|--------|------|---|
| (He is) | He's | |
| (She is) | She's | |
| (It is) | It's | in the kitchen. |
| (We are) | We're | |
| (You are) | You're | |
| (They are) | They're | |

Where are you?

I'm in the kitchen.

Where are you?

We're in the living room.

Where are Mr. and Mrs. Jones?

They're in the yard.

1. Where are you?

   I'm in the bedroom

2. Where are you?

   We're in the kitchen

3. Where are Jim and Pam?

   They're in the living room

4. Where are you?

   I'm in the bathroom

5. Where are Mr. and Mrs. Park?

   They're in the dining room

6. Where are you?

   They are in the yard.

7. Where are you?

   I'm in the garage

8. Where are you and Ben?

   They're in the basement

9. Where are Mr. and Mrs. Hernandez?

   They're in the attic

11

# Where's Bob?

*Where's = Where is

**1.** Where's Tim?

He's in the bedroom

**2.** Where's Rosa?

She's in the yard

**3.** Where's the newspaper?

It's on the table

**4.** Where's Peggy?

**5.** Where's the telephone book?

It's on the bed

**6.** Where's Harry?

He's in the bathroom

**7.** Where's Ellen?

She's in the livingroom

**8.** Where's Kevin?

He's in the Garage

**9.** Where's the cell phone?

It's on the table

## THE STUDENTS IN MY ENGLISH CLASS

The students in my English class are very interesting. Henry is Chinese. He's from Shanghai. Linda is Puerto Rican. She's from San Juan. Mr. and Mrs. Kim are Korean. They're from Seoul.

George is Greek. He's from Athens. Carla is Italian. She's from Rome. Mr. and Mrs. Sato are Japanese. They're from Tokyo. My friend Maria and I are Mexican. We're from Mexico City.

Yes, the students in my English class are very interesting. We're from many different countries . . . and we're friends.

✔ **READING** *CHECK-UP*

### TRUE OR FALSE?

F   **1.** Linda is Korean.

T   **2.** George is Greek.

F   **3.** Henry is from Mexico City.

T   **4.** Mr. Kim is from Seoul.

F   **5.** Carla is Chinese.

T   **6.** The students in the class are from many countries.

### How About You?

Tell about the students in YOUR English class. Where are they from?

# How to Say It!

### Greeting People

**A.** Hi. How are you?
**B.** Fine. And you?
**A.** Fine, thanks.

**Practice conversations with other students.**

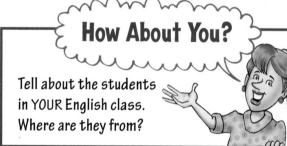

# Where Are They?

*donde*

**Ask and answer questions based on these pictures.**

1. Where is Albert?
He is in the Restaurant.

2. Where is Carmen?
She is in the Bank.

3. Where are Walter and Mary?
They are in the super market.

4. Where are you?
I am in the library

5. Where are you?
We are in the Park.

6. Where is Kate?
She is in the movie theater.

7. Where are Mr. and Mrs. Lee?
They are in Post Office

8. Where is the monkey?
It is in the ZOO.

9. Where am I?
x. I am in the Hospital.

**Now add people and places of your own.**

10. Where is my dog?
It is in my yard.

11. Where is my cat?
It is in my living room.

12. Where is my bird?
It is in My Kitchen.

14

# READING

George

Maria

Mr. and Mrs. Sato

our English teacher

## ALL THE STUDENTS IN MY ENGLISH CLASS ARE ABSENT TODAY

All the students in my English class are absent today. George is absent. He's in the hospital. Maria is absent. She's at the dentist. Mr. and Mrs. Sato are absent. They're at the social security office. Even our English teacher is absent. He's home in bed!

What a shame! Everybody in my English class is absent today. Everybody except me.

✔ **READING** *CHECK-UP*

### WHAT'S THE ANSWER?

1. Where's George?
2. Where's Maria?
3. Where are Mr. and Mrs. Sato?
4. Where's the English teacher?

## How About You?

Tell about YOUR English class:
Which students are in class today?
Which students are absent today?
Where are they?

# LISTENING

### WHAT'S THE WORD?

Listen and choose the correct answer.

1. a. bank          b. park
2. a. hospital      b. library
3. a. He's          b. She's
4. a. He's          b. She's
5. a. We're         b. They're
6. a. We're         b. They're

### WHERE ARE THEY?

Listen and choose the correct place.

1. a. living room   b. dining room
2. a. bathroom      b. bedroom
3. a. garage        b. yard
4. a. bathroom      b. bedroom
5. a. kitchen       b. living room
6. a. bedroom       b. basement

15

## PRONUNCIATION  Reduced *and*

> Mr. and Mrs.

**Listen.  Then say it.**

Mr. and Mrs. Jones

Mr. and Mrs. Park

Jim and Pam

You and Ben

**Say it.  Then listen.**

Mr. and Mrs. Lee

Mr. and Mrs. Miller

Walter and Mary

Jim and I

**SIDE by SIDE JOURNAL**
Draw a picture of your apartment or house. Label the rooms.

**Project**
Work with another student. Draw a picture of your classroom. Label all the objects.

# CHAPTER SUMMARY

## GRAMMAR

### SUBJECT PRONOUNS
### TO BE + LOCATION

| | am | I? |
|---|---|---|
| | is | he? she? it? |
| Where | are | we? you? they? |

| | | |
|---|---|---|
| (I am) | I'm | |
| (He is) | He's | |
| (She is) | She's | |
| (It is) | It's | in the kitchen. |
| (We are) | We're | |
| (You are) | You're | |
| (They are) | They're | |

## KEY VOCABULARY

### CLASSROOM OBJECTS

board
book
bookshelf
bulletin board
chair
clock
computer
desk
dictionary
globe
map
notebook
pen
pencil
ruler
table
wall

### PLACES AT HOME

attic
basement
bathroom
bedroom
dining room
garage
kitchen
living room
yard

### PLACES AROUND TOWN

bank
hospital
library
movie theater
park
post office
restaurant
supermarket
zoo

### GREETING PEOPLE

Hi.  How are you?
    Fine.  And you?
Fine, thanks.

# 3

# Present Continuous Tense

- **Everyday Activities**

**VOCABULARY PREVIEW**

1. eating
2. drinking
3. cooking
4. reading
5. studying

6. teaching
7. singing
8. sleeping
9. swimming
10. planting

11. watching TV
12. listening to music
13. playing cards
14. playing baseball
15. playing the piano

# What Are You Doing?

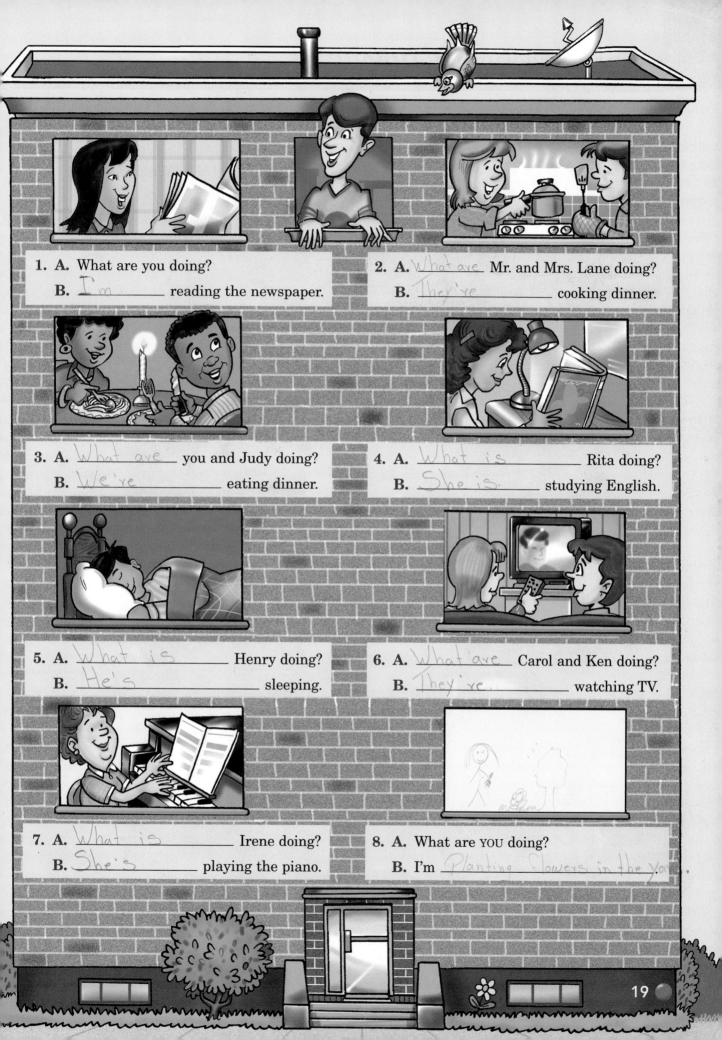

1. A. What are you doing?
   B. I'm _____ reading the newspaper.

2. A. What are _____ Mr. and Mrs. Lane doing?
   B. They're _____ cooking dinner.

3. A. What are _____ you and Judy doing?
   B. We're _____ eating dinner.

4. A. What is _____ Rita doing?
   B. She is. _____ studying English.

5. A. What is _____ Henry doing?
   B. He's _____ sleeping.

6. A. What are _____ Carol and Ken doing?
   B. They're _____ watching TV.

7. A. What is _____ Irene doing?
   B. She's _____ playing the piano.

8. A. What are YOU doing?
   B. I'm _Planting flowers in the yard._

# What's Everybody Doing?

7/15/2014

A. Where's Walter?

B. He's in the kitchen.

A. What's he doing?

B. He's eating breakfast.

Where's
She's

**1.** *Karen*
*park*
*eating lunch*

**2.** *Mr. and Mrs. Clark*
*dining room*
*eating dinner*

**3.** *you*
*bedroom*
*playing the guitar*

**4.** *you*
*living room*
*playing cards*

**5.** *Gary and Jane*
*yard*
*playing baseball*

**6.** *Miss Baker*
*cafeteria*
*drinking milk*

**7.** *you*
*library*
*studying English*

**8.** *Ms. Johnson*
*classroom*
*teaching mathematics*

**9.** *Marvin*
*bathroom*
*singing*

**10.** *Martha*
*hospital*
*watching TV*

She's

**11.** *your friend*
*park*
*listening to music*

**12.** Audel
Kitchen
home work

Action Game!

What am I doing?

You're playing the guitar.

Pantomime an everyday activity for the class. Ask students, "What am I doing?"

# READING

## IN THE PARK

The Jones family is in the park today. The sun is shining, and the birds are singing. It's a beautiful day!

Mr. Jones is reading the newspaper. Mrs. Jones is listening to the radio. Sally and Patty Jones are studying. And Tommy Jones is playing the guitar.

The Jones family is very happy today. It's a beautiful day, and they're in the park.

## AT HOME IN THE YARD

The Chen family is at home in the yard today. The sun is shining, and the birds are singing. It's a beautiful day!

Mr. Chen is planting flowers. Mrs. Chen is drinking lemonade and reading a book. Emily and Jason Chen are playing with the dog. And Jennifer Chen is sleeping.

The Chen family is very happy today. It's a beautiful day, and they're at home in the yard.

# ✔ READING CHECK-UP

## TRUE OR FALSE?

___F___ 1. The Jones family is at home in the yard today.

___F___ 2. Mrs. Chen is planting flowers.

___T___ 3. Patty Jones is studying.

___F___ 4. Jason Chen is reading a book.

___F___ 5. The Chen family is singing.

___T___ 6. The Jones family and the Chen family are very happy today.

## Q & A

Using this model, make questions and answers based on the stories on page 22.

**A.** *What's Mr. Jones doing?*
**B.** *He's reading the newspaper.*

## LISTENING

Listen and choose the correct answer.

1. a. She's studying.
   b. I'm studying.

2. a. He's eating.
   b. She's eating.

3. a. He's watching TV.
   b. She's watching TV.

4. a. We're cooking dinner.
   b. They're cooking dinner.

5. a. We're planting flowers.
   b. They're planting flowers.

6. a. You're playing baseball.
   b. We're playing baseball.

## IN YOUR OWN WORDS

### FOR WRITING AND DISCUSSION

Mr. and Mrs. Martinez

Alex Martinez

Tina Martinez

Jimmy Martinez

**AT THE BEACH**

The Martinez family is at the beach today. Using this picture, tell a story about the Martinez family.

## PRONUNCIATION  Reduced *What are* & *Where are*

**Listen. Then say it.**

What are you doing?

What are Jim and Jane doing?

Where are Mary and Fred?

Where are you and Judy?

**Say it. Then listen.**

What are they doing?

What are Carol and Ken doing?

Where are Mr. and Mrs. Lane?

Where are you and Henry?

SIDE by SIDE JOURNAL

What are you doing now?
What are your friends doing?
Write about it in your
journal.

## CHAPTER SUMMARY

### GRAMMAR

**PRESENT CONTINUOUS TENSE**

| What | am | I | doing? |
|------|-----|-----------------|--------|
|      | is  | he she it       |        |
|      | are | we you they     |        |

| (I am)     | I'm     | eating. |
|------------|---------|---------|
| (He is)    | He's    |         |
| (She is)   | She's   |         |
| (It is)    | It's    |         |
| (We are)   | We're   |         |
| (You are)  | You're  |         |
| (They are) | They're |         |

### KEY VOCABULARY

**EVERYDAY ACTIVITIES**

cooking dinner
drinking milk/lemonade
eating breakfast/lunch/dinner
listening to music/the radio
planting flowers
playing cards
playing baseball
playing the guitar/the piano

reading a book/the newspaper
singing
sleeping
studying English
swimming
teaching
watching TV

**CHECKING UNDERSTANDING**

*In the kitchen?*

## FACT FILE

**Titles**

**Mr.** is a title for a man.
**Ms., Mrs.,** and **Miss** are titles for a woman.

*Mistress*

**Nicknames**

My name is David.
My nickname is Dave.

### COMMON NICKNAMES

| Name | Nickname | Name | Nickname |
|------|----------|------|----------|
| James | Jim | Elizabeth | Liz, Betty |
| Peter | Pete | Jennifer | Jenny |
| Robert | Bob | Judith | Judy |
| Timothy | Tim | Katherine | Kathy, Kate |
| Thomas | Tom | Patricia | Patty |
| William | Bill | Susan | Sue |

## Global Exchange

**SungHee:** Hello. My name is Sung Hee. I'm Korean. I'm from Seoul. I'm a student. Right now I'm in my English class. I'm looking for a keypal in a different country.

**DanielR:** Hi, Sung Hee! My name is Daniel. My nickname is Danny. My last name is Rivera. I'm Mexican. I'm from Mexico City. I'm a student. Right now I'm at home. I'm at my computer, and I'm listening to music. I'm also looking for a keypal. Tell me about your school and your English class.

**Send a message over the Internet. Tell about yourself. Look for a keypal.**

## BUILD YOUR VOCABULARY!
Playing Instruments, Sports, and Games

I'm playing _____ .

**Instruments**
- the violin
- the clarinet
- the trumpet

**Sports**
- soccer
- tennis
- basketball

**Games**
- chess
- checkers
- tic tac toe

## AROUND THE WORLD

### Greetings

**R**ight now, all around the world, people are greeting each other in different ways.

They're shaking hands.

They're kissing.

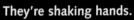
sequiring

They're bowing.

They're hugging.

bowing↑

How are people in your country greeting each other today?

---

## LISTENING

You have seven messages!

## You Have Seven Messages!

Messages

| | | |
|---|---|---|
| _c_ | ① | **a.** Mrs. Lane  731–0248 |
| ___ | ② | **b.** Linda Lee  969–0159 |
| ___ | ③ | **c.** Henry Drake  427–9168 |
| ___ | ④ | **d.** Dad |
| ___ | ⑤ | **e.** Patty |
| ___ | ⑥ | **f.** Jim  682–4630 |
| ___ | ⑦ | **g.** Kevin Carter  298–4577 |

## What Are They Saying?

WELCOME

---

# To Be: Short Answers
# Possessive Adjectives

- **Everyday Activities**

## Vocabulary Preview

FEED

1. brushing
2. cleaning
3. feeding
4. fixing
5. painting
6. reading
7. washing

# I'm Fixing My Sink

| I | my |
|---|---|
| he | his |
| she | her |
| it | its |
| we | our |
| you | your |
| they | their |

Hi! What are you doing?

I'm fixing **my** sink.

What's Bob doing?

He's fixing **his** car.

What's Mary doing?

She's cleaning **her** room.

What are you doing?

We're cleaning **our** apartment.

What are **your** children doing?

They're doing **their** homework.

# Are You Busy?

|  | | |
|---|---|---|
| Yes, | I | am. |
| | he<br>she<br>it | is. |
| | we<br>you<br>they | are. |

**Are you busy?**

**Yes, I am.**
**I'm washing my hair.**

1. Is Frank busy?
   *He's cleaning his apartment*

2. Is Helen busy?
   *She feeding her cat*

3. Are you busy?
   *WE're fixing our TV*

4. Are Jim and Lisa busy?
   *They're painting their bedroom*

5. Are you busy?
   *I'm doing my homework*

6. Is Richard busy?
   *He's washing his clothes*

**7.** Are Ed and Ruth busy?

*They're painting their garage*

**8.** Is Timmy busy?

*He's feeding his dog*

**9.** Are you busy?

*We're doing our exercises*

**10.** Are you busy?

*I'm fixing my bicycle*

**11.** Is Karen busy?

*She's washing her car*

**12.** Is Anwar busy?

*He's cleaning his yard*

**13.** Are your children busy?

*They're brushing their teeth*

**14.** Are you busy?

*We're washing our windows*

**15.** Is Wendy busy?

*She's reading her e-mail*

## How to Say It!

**Attracting Someone's Attention**

A. Jane?
B. Yes?
A. What are you doing?
B. I'm *doing my exercises.*

**Practice conversations with other students.**

# TALK ABOUT IT! *Where Are They, and What Are They Doing?*

Use these models to talk about the picture with other students in your class.

**A.** Where's *Mr. Molina*?

**B.** *He's* in the *park*.

**A.** What's *he* doing?

**B.** *He's listening to the radio.*

**A.** Where are *Mr. and Mrs. Sharp*?

**B.** They're in the *laundromat*.

**A.** What are they doing?

**B.** They're *washing their clothes*.

# READING

## A BUSY DAY

Mr. Price
Ms. Hunter
Ricky Gomez
Mr. and Mrs. Wong
me
RIVER STREET
159
Mrs. Martin
Judy and Larry Clark

Everybody at 159 River Street is very busy today. Mr. Price is cleaning his bedroom. Ms. Hunter is painting her bathroom. Ricky Gomez is feeding his cat. Mr. and Mrs. Wong are washing their clothes. Mrs. Martin is doing her exercises. And Judy and Larry Clark are fixing their car.

I'm busy, too. I'm washing my windows . . . and of course, I'm watching all my neighbors. It's a very busy day at 159 River Street.

## ✔ READING CHECK-UP

### TRUE OR FALSE?

___ 1. Mr. Price is in his bedroom.

___ 2. Ricky is eating.

___ 3. Mr. and Mrs. Clark are in their apartment.

___ 4. Mrs. Martin is doing her exercises.

___ 5. Their address is 195 River Street.

### Q & A

**Using this model, make questions and answers based on the story.**

A. *What's Mr. Price doing?*
B. *He's cleaning his bedroom.*

# LISTENING

**Listen and choose the correct answer.**

1. a. The newspaper.
   b. Breakfast.

2. a. Her e-mail.
   b. Dinner.

3. a. The dining room.
   b. Soccer.

4. a. Their kitchen.
   b. Basketball.

5. a. TV.
   b. My clothes.

6. a. His neighbors.
   b. His windows.

# IN YOUR OWN WORDS

### FOR WRITING AND DISCUSSION

09/26

## A BUSY DAY

Everybody at 320 Main Street is very busy today. Tell a story about them, using this picture and the story on page 32 as a guide.

their There they're paint

33

## PRONUNCIATION  Deleted *h*

**Listen.  Then say it.**

She's fixing her car.

She's cleaning her room.

He's feeding his dog.

He's washing his windows.

**Say it.  Then listen.**

He's painting his apartment.

She's doing her homework.

He's brushing his teeth.

She's reading her e-mail.

Go to a place in your community—a park, a library, a supermarket, or someplace else.  Look at the people. What are they doing?  Write about it in your journal.

# CHAPTER SUMMARY

## GRAMMAR

### TO BE: SHORT ANSWERS

| | | |
|---|---|---|
| | I | am. |
| | he she it | is. |
| Yes, | we you they | are. |

### POSSESSIVE ADJECTIVES

| | | | |
|---|---|---|---|
| I'm He's She's It's We're You're They're | cleaning | my his her its our your their | room. |

## KEY VOCABULARY

### EVERYDAY ACTIVITIES

brushing *my* teeth
cleaning *his* apartment / garage / living room / room / yard
doing *her* exercises / homework
feeding *our* cat / dog
fixing *your* bicycle / car / sink / TV
painting *their* bathroom / bedroom / kitchen / living room
washing *my* car / clothes / hair / windows

### GREETING PEOPLE

Hi!

### ATTRACTING ATTENTION

*Jane?*

# 5

## To Be: Yes/No Questions
## Short Answers
## Adjectives
## Possessive Nouns

• **Describing People and Things**  •  **Weather**

### VOCABULARY PREVIEW

| | | |
|---|---|---|
| **1.** tall – short | **5.** married – single | **9.** noisy/loud – quiet |
| **2.** young – old | **6.** handsome – ugly | **10.** expensive – cheap |
| **3.** heavy/fat – thin | **7.** beautiful/pretty – ugly | **11.** easy – difficult |
| **4.** new – old | **8.** large/big – small/little | **12.** rich – poor |

# Tall or Short?

| | |
|---|---|
| (I am) | I'm |
| (He is) | He's |
| (She is) | She's |
| (It is) | It's |
| (We are) | We're |
| (You are) | You're |
| (They are) | They're |

tall.

Bob    Bill

**A.** Is Bob tall or short?

**B.** He's tall.

**A.** Is Bill tall or short?

**B.** He's short.

---

**Ask and answer these questions.**

Kate    Peggy

1. Is Kate young or old?
2. Is Peggy young or old?

Howard    Mike

3. Is Howard heavy or thin?
4. Is Mike fat or thin?

Howard's car    Mike's car

5. Is Howard's car new or old?
6. Is Mike's car new or old?

Gloria    Jennifer

7. Is Gloria married or single?
8. Is Jennifer married or single?

Robert *handsom* Captain Crook

*ugly*

9. Is Robert handsome or ugly?

10. Is Captain Crook handsome or ugly?

Vanessa *beautifu* Hilda *ugly*

11. Is Vanessa beautiful or ugly?

12. Is Hilda pretty or ugly?

*large* *small*

Robert's house George's apartment

13. Is Robert's house large or small?

14. Is George's apartment big or little?

*noisy* *quiet*

Kate's neighbors Peggy's neighbors

15. Are Kate's neighbors noisy or quiet?

16. Are Peggy's neighbors loud or quiet?

*Expensive* *cheap*

the food at the Plaza Restaurant | the food at Burger Town

17. Is the food at the Plaza Restaurant expensive or cheap?

18. Is the food at Burger Town expensive or cheap?

*easy* *difficult*

the questions in Chapter 5 | the questions in Chapter 17

19. Are the questions in Chapter 5 easy or difficult?

20. Are the questions in Chapter 17 easy or difficult?

*rich*

Marvin Larry

*poor*

21. Is Marvin rich or poor?

22. Is Larry rich or poor?

*sad* *happy*

*Sam* *Jane*

**Now ask and answer your own questions.**

*Is Sam happy or sad*
*Is Jane happy or sad.*

# Tell Me About . . .

question

| Am | I | | |
|----|---|---|---|
| Is | he<br>she<br>it | | tall? |
| Are | we<br>you<br>they | | |

answer

| | | I | am. |
|---|---|---|---|
| Yes, | | he<br>she<br>it | is. |
| | | we<br>you<br>they | are. |

negative answer

| | | I'm | not. |
|---|---|---|---|
| No, | | he<br>she<br>it | isn't. |
| | | we<br>you<br>they | aren't. |

**Are you married?**

**No, I'm not. I'm single.**

**Tell me about your new car. Is it large?**

**No, it isn't. It's small.**

**Tell me about your new neighbors. Are they quiet?**

**No, they aren't. They're noisy.**

1. **A.** Tell me about your computer.
   Is it _____ new?
   **B.** No, _it isn't_. _it's old_.

2. **A.** Tell me about your new boss.
   Is he _____ young?
   **B.** No, _he isn't_. _he is old_.

38

**3. A.** Tell me about your neighbors.
<u>Are they</u> noisy?
**B.** No, <u>they aren't</u>. <u>they're they are quiet</u>.

**4. A.** Tell me about the Plaza Restaurant.
<u>Is it</u> cheap?
**B.** No, <u>it isn't</u>. <u>It is expensive</u>.

**5. A.** Tell me about your brother.
<u>Is he</u> tall?
**B.** No, <u>he isn't</u>. <u>he is short</u>.

**6. A.** Tell me about your sister.
<u>Is she</u> single?
**B.** No, <u>she isn't</u>. <u>She is married</u>.

**7. A.** Tell me about Nancy's cat.
<u>Is it</u> pretty?
**B.** No, <u>it isn't</u>. <u>it is ugly</u>.

**8. A.** Tell me about Ron and Betty's dog.
<u>Is it</u> little?
**B.** No, <u>it isn't</u>. <u>it is big</u>.

**9. A.** Tell me about the questions in your English book.
<u>Are they</u> difficult?
**B.** No, <u>they aren't</u>. <u>they are easy</u>.

**10. A.** Tell me about Santa Claus.
<u>Is he</u> thin?
**B.** No, <u>he isn't</u>. <u>he is fat</u>.

# How's the Weather Today? *it's bowl*

How's the weather today in YOUR city?

## How to Say It!

**Calling Someone You Know on the Telephone**

A. Hello.
B. Hello. Is this *Julie*?
A. Yes, it is.
B. Hi, *Julie*. This is *Anna*.
A. Hi, *Anna*. . . .

Practice conversations with other students.

# The Weather Is Terrible Here!

A. Hi, Jack. This is Jim. I'm calling from Miami.

B. From Miami? What are you doing in Miami?

A. I'm on ~~vacation.~~

B. How's the weather in Miami? Is it sunny?

A. No, it isn't. It's raining.

B. Is it hot?

A. No, it isn't. It's cold.

B. Are you having a good time?

A. No, I'm not. I'm having a TERRIBLE time.
The weather is TERRIBLE here!

B. I'm sorry to hear that.

hurricane

---

A. Hi, _Jack_. This is _Jim_. I'm calling from _Miami_.

B. From _Miami_? What are you doing in _Miami_?

A. I'm on vacation.

B. How's the weather in _Miami_? Is it _sunny_?    *How is*

A. No, it isn't. It's _raining_.    *it's not*

B. Is it _hot_?

A. No, it isn't. It's _cold_.

B. Are you having a good time?

A. No, I'm not. I'm having a TERRIBLE time. The weather is TERRIBLE here!

B. I'm sorry to hear that.

---

1. *British Columbia*
   *cool?*
   *snowing?*

2. *Tahiti*
   *hot?*
   *sunny?*

You're on vacation, and the weather is terrible! Call a student in your class. Use the conversation above as a guide.

### DEAR MOTHER

## Royal Sludge Hotel

*idiom*

Dear Mother,

I'm writing from our hotel at Sludge Beach. Ralph and I are on vacation with the children for a few days. We're happy to be here, but to tell the truth, we're having a few problems.

The weather isn't very good. In fact, it's cold and cloudy. Right now I'm looking out the window, and it's raining cats and dogs.

The children aren't very happy. In fact, they're bored and they're having a terrible time. Right now they're sitting on the bed, playing tic tac toe and watching TV.

The restaurants here are expensive, and the food isn't very good. In fact, Ralph is at a clinic right now. He's having problems with his stomach.

All the other hotels here are beautiful and new.  Our hotel is ugly, and it's very, very old.  In fact, right now a repairperson is fixing the bathroom sink.

So, Mother, we're having a few problems here at Sludge Beach, but we're happy.  We're happy to be on vacation, and we're happy to be together.

See you soon.

Love,

Ethel

## ✔ READING *CHECK-UP*

### TRUE OR FALSE?

____ **1.** The weather is beautiful.

____ **2.** The children are happy.

____ **3.** The children are watching TV.

____ **4.** The restaurants are cheap.

____ **5.** Ralph is at the hotel right now.

____ **6.** Their hotel is old.

____ **7.** A repairperson is fixing the window.

____ **8.** Ethel is watching the cats and dogs.

## LISTENING

### WHAT'S THE ANSWER?

Listen and choose the correct answer.

**1.** a. It's large.     b. It's heavy.
**2.** a. It's married.   b. It's beautiful.
**3.** a. They're quiet.  b. They're sunny.
**4.** a. It's young.     b. It's warm.
**5.** a. It's small.     b. It's easy.
**6.** a. It's good.      b. It's raining.

### TRUE OR FALSE?

Listen to the conversation.  Then answer *True* or *False*.

**1.** Louise is calling Betty.
**2.** The weather is hot and sunny.
**3.** The hotel is old.
**4.** The food is very good.
**5.** Louise is watching TV.

43

**Listen.  Then say it.**

Is Bob tall or short?

Is Kate young or old?

Are they noisy or quiet?

Is it hot or cold?

**Say it.  Then listen.**

Is the car new or old?

Are you married or single?

Is it sunny or cloudy?

Are they large or small?

**SIDE by SIDE JOURNAL**

How's the weather today?
What are you doing now?
Write a letter to a friend
and tell about it.

May 20, 20__

Dear ___,

_____

Sincerely,

---

# CHAPTER SUMMARY

## GRAMMAR

### To Be: Yes / No Questions

| Am | I | |
|---|---|---|
| Is | he she it | tall? |
| Are | we you they | |

*(handwritten marks: 1S, 3S, 2nd)*

### To Be: Short Answers

| | I | am. |
|---|---|---|
| Yes, | he she it | is. |
| | we you they | are. |

| | I'm | not. |
|---|---|---|
| No, | he she it | isn't. |
| | we you they | aren't. |

### Possessive Nouns

Robert's house

Peggy's neighbors

George's apartment

*WRITE A STORY FOR HOMEWORK*

## KEY VOCABULARY

### Describing People and Things

| | | | |
|---|---|---|---|
| tall | short | large | small |
| young | old | big | little |
| new | old | noisy/loud | quiet |
| heavy/fat | thin | expensive | cheap |
| married | single | easy | difficult |
| handsome | ugly | rich | poor |
| beautiful/pretty | ugly | | |

### Weather

It's sunny.     It's hot.

It's cloudy.    It's warm.

It's raining.   It's cool.

It's snowing.   It's cold.

# To Be: Review
# Present Continuous Tense: Review
# Prepositions of Location

- **Family Members**
- **Describing Activities and Events**

## VOCABULARY PREVIEW

| | | | | |
|---|---|---|---|---|
| 1. wife | **children** | **grandparents** | **grandchildren** | 13. aunt |
| 2. husband | 5. daughter | 9. grandmother | 11. granddaughter | 14. uncle |
| | 6. son | 10. grandfather | 12. grandson | 15. niece |
| **parents** | 7. sister | | | 16. nephew |
| 3. mother | 8. brother | | | 17. cousin |
| 4. father | | | | |

# My Favorite Photographs

**A.** Who is he?

**B.** He's my father.

**A.** What's his name?

**B.** His name is Paul.

**A.** Where is he?

**B.** He's in Paris.

**A.** What's he doing?

**B.** He's standing in front of the Eiffel Tower.

---

Using these questions, talk about the following photographs.

*fotografs*

*quien*

| | | |
|---|---|---|
| Who is he? | Who is she? | Who are they? |
| What's his name? | What's her name? | What are their names? |
| Where is he? | Where is she? | Where are they? |
| What's he doing? | What's she doing? | What are they doing? |

**1.** *my mother*
*in the park*
*riding her bicycle*

**2.** *my parents*
*in the dining room*
*having dinner*

**3.** *my son*
*at the beach*
*swimming*

**4.** *my daughter*
*in front of our house*
*washing her car*

**5.** *my wife*
*in the yard*
*planting flowers*

**6.** *my husband*
*in our living room*
*sleeping on the sofa*

**7.** *my sister and brother*
*in the kitchen*
*baking a cake*

**8.** *my grandmother and grandfather*
*at my wedding*
*crying*

**9.** *my aunt and uncle*
*in Washington, D.C.*
*standing in front of the White House*

**10.** *my cousin*
*in front of his apartment building*
*skateboarding*

**11.** *my niece*
*at school*
*acting in a play*

**12.** *my nephew*
*in his bedroom*
*sitting on his bed and playing the guitar*

**13.** *my friend*
*in his apartment*
*playing a game on his computer*

**14.** *my friends*
*at my birthday party*
*singing and dancing*

## ON YOUR OWN *Your Favorite Photographs*

This is a photograph of my sister and me. My sister's name is Amanda. We're in the park. Amanda is feeding the birds, and I'm sitting on a bench and listening to music.

Bring in your favorite photographs to class. Talk about them with other students. Ask the other students about *their* favorite photographs.

# READING

*[handwritten annotations: barking / ladrar, argueing / pelea, fighting / pelea, vacuuming · aspiradora (sucking)]*

## ARTHUR IS VERY ANGRY

It's late at night. Arthur is sitting on his bed, and he's looking at his clock. His neighbors are making a lot of noise, and Arthur is VERY angry.

The people in Apartment 2 are dancing. The man in Apartment 3 is vacuuming his rug. The woman in Apartment 4 is playing the drums. The teenagers in Apartment 5 are listening to loud music. The dog in Apartment 6 is barking. And the people in Apartment 7 are having a big argument.

It's very late, and Arthur is tired and angry. What a terrible night!

## ✔ READING CHECK-UP

### Q & A

Using this model, make questions and answers based on the story.

**A.** *What's the man in Apartment 3 doing?*
**B.** *He's vacuuming his rugs.*

### CHOOSE

1. Arthur's neighbors are _____.
   a. noisy
   b. angry

2. The man in Apartment 3 is _____.
   a. painting
   b. cleaning

3. The people in Apartment 5 are _____.
   a. young
   b. old

4. The dog in Apartment 6 isn't _____.
   a. sleeping
   b. making noise

5. The woman in Apartment 4 is _____.
   a. playing cards
   b. playing music

6. Arthur isn't very _____.
   a. happy
   b. tired

# READING

## TOM'S WEDDING DAY

Today is a very special day. It's my wedding day, and all my family and friends are here. Everybody is having a wonderful time.

*chimenea*

*bestido* / *gaun*

My wife, Jane, is standing in front of the fireplace. She's wearing a beautiful white wedding gown. Uncle Harry is taking her photograph, and Aunt Emma is crying. (She's very sentimental.)

The band is playing my favorite popular music. My mother is dancing with Jane's father, and Jane's mother is dancing with my father.

My sister and Jane's brother are standing in the yard and eating wedding cake. Our grandparents are sitting in the corner and talking about "the good old days."

Everybody is having a good time. People are singing, dancing, and laughing, and our families are getting to know each other. It's a very special day.

## ✔ READING *CHECK-UP*

### WHAT'S THE ANSWER?

*standing*

1. Where is Jane standing?
2. What's she wearing?
3. What's Uncle Harry doing?

4. What's Aunt Emma doing?
5. What's Tom's mother doing?
6. What are their grandparents doing?

# LISTENING

## QUIET OR NOISY?

Listen to the sentence. Are the people quiet or noisy?

1. a. quiet      b. noisy
2. a. quiet      b. noisy
3. a. quiet      b. noisy
4. a. quiet      b. noisy
5. a. quiet      b. noisy
6. a. quiet      b. noisy

## WHAT DO YOU HEAR?

Listen to the sound. What do you hear? Choose the correct answer.

1. a. They're studying.      b. They're singing.
2. a. He's crying.      b. He's doing his exercises.
3. a. She's vacuuming.      b. She's washing her clothes.
4. a. They're barking.      b. They're laughing.
5. a. She's playing the piano.      b. She's playing the drums.

# IN YOUR OWN WORDS

FOR WRITING AND DISCUSSION

### JESSICA'S BIRTHDAY PARTY

Today is a very special day. It's Jessica's birthday party, and all her family and friends are there. Using this picture, tell a story about her party.

## How to Say It!

### Introducing People

A. I'd like to introduce *my brother*.
B. Nice to meet you.
C. Nice to meet you, too.

**Practice conversations with other students.**

# PRONUNCIATION  *Stressed and Unstressed Words*

**Listen.  Then say it.**

He's pláying the guitár.

She's ácting in a pláy.

She's ríding her bícycle.

He's sleéping on the sófa.

**Say it.  Then listen.**

We're báking a cáke.

They're sítting in the yárd.

He's wáshing his cár.

She's sítting on her béd.

**SIDE by SIDE JOURNAL**

Write in your journal about your favorite photograph.

This is a photograph of _____.

In this photograph, _____.

It's my favorite photograph because _____.

# CHAPTER SUMMARY

## GRAMMAR

### TO BE

| Who is | he? she? |
|--------|----------|
| Who are | they? |

| He's my father. She's my wife. |
|---|
| They're my parents. |

### PRESENT CONTINUOUS TENSE

| What's | he she | doing? |
|--------|--------|--------|
| What are | they | doing? |

| He's She's | sleeping. |
|------------|-----------|
| They're | swimming. |

### PREPOSITIONS OF LOCATION

| She's **in** the park. | He's sitting **on** his bed. |
|---|---|
| He's **at** the beach. | We're **in front of** our house. |

## KEY VOCABULARY

**FAMILY MEMBERS**

| mother | grandmother | wife |
|--------|-------------|------|
| father | grandfather | husband |
| parents | grandparents | aunt |
| son | grandson | uncle |
| daughter | granddaughter | niece |
| children | grandchildren | nephew |
| brother | sister | cousin |

**EVERYDAY ACTIVITIES**

| acting | laughing |
|--------|----------|
| baking | riding |
| crying | skateboarding |
| dancing | talking |
| having *dinner* | vacuuming |

**INTRODUCING SOMEONE**

I'd like to introduce _____.
  Nice to meet you.
    Nice to meet you, too.

**BUILD YOUR VOCABULARY!**

Classroom Activities

*I'm _____ .*

## A Family Tree

*here*
*her*

Betty and Henry Wilson's family tree is very large

*daughter-in-law*

- ■ reading
- ■ writing
- ■ raising my hand
- ■ opening my book
- ■ closing my book
- ■ erasing the board
- ■ using a calculator

A family tree is a diagram of the people in a family. This is the Wilson family tree. All the members of the Wilson family are on this family tree—parents, children, grandparents, grandchildren, aunts, uncles, cousins, nieces, and nephews.

Betty and Henry are the parents of Sally, Linda, and Tom. Linda is single. Sally is married. Her husband's name is Jack. Sally and Jack are the parents of Jimmy and Sarah. Jimmy is their son, and Sarah is their daughter.

Tom is also married. His wife's name is Patty. Patty and Tom are the parents of Julie and Kevin. Julie is their daughter, and Kevin is their son.

Jimmy, Sarah, Julie, and Kevin are cousins. They are also the grandchildren of Betty and Henry. (Betty and Henry are their grandparents.)

Jack is Julie and Kevin's uncle. Sally is their aunt. Tom is Jimmy and Sarah's uncle. Patty is their aunt. Linda is also the aunt of Jimmy, Sarah, Julie, and Kevin.

Jimmy is the nephew of Linda, Patty, and Tom. Sarah is their niece. Julie is the niece of Sally, Jack, and Linda. Kevin is their nephew.

*Draw your family tree. Then write about it.*

## Today's Weather

| | | | | | |
|---|---|---|---|---|---|
| _d_ | ① | hot | a. | Atlanta |
| _b_ | ② | snowing | b. | Chicago |
| ___ | ③ | warm and sunny | c. | Toronto |
| ___ | ④ | cool and sunny | d. | Honolulu |
| ___ | ⑤ | cold and cloudy | e. | Los Angeles |

## AROUND THE WORLD

### Extended and Nuclear Families

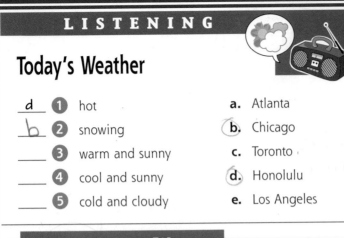

This is an **extended family**. The grandparents, parents, and children are all together in one apartment. An uncle, an aunt, and two cousins are in another apartment in the same building. Extended families are very common around the world.

This is a **nuclear family**. Only the mother, father, and children are in this home. The grandparents, aunts, uncles, and cousins are in different homes. Nuclear families are very common in many countries.

Is your family a nuclear family or an extended family? Which type of family is common in your country? In your opinion, what are some good things and bad things about these different types of families?

## Global Exchange

**Ken425:** It's a beautiful day in our city today. It's warm and sunny. The people in my family are very busy. My brother and sister are cleaning our apartment. My mother is washing the windows, and my father is fixing the bathroom sink. I'm cooking dinner for my family. How about you? What's the weather today? What are you doing? What are other people in your family doing?

Send a message to a keypal. Tell about the weather, and tell about what you and others are doing today.

## FACT FILE

### Family Relationships

| | | |
|---|---|---|
| wife's mother<br>husband's mother } | = | mother-in-law |
| wife's father<br>husband's father } | = | father-in-law |
| son's wife | = | daughter-in-law |
| daughter's husband | = | son-in-law |
| wife's sister<br>husband's sister } | = | sister-in-law |
| wife's brother<br>husband's brother } | = | brother-in-law |

## What Are They Saying?

# 7

## Prepositions
## There Is/There Are
## Singular/Plural: Introduction

- Places Around Town
- Locating Places
- Describing Neighborhoods
- Describing Apartments

### VOCABULARY PREVIEW

1. bakery
2. barber shop
3. book store
4. bus station
5. cafeteria
6. clinic
7. department store
8. drug store
9. hair salon
10. health club
11. hotel
12. laundromat
13. school
14. train station
15. video store

# Where's the Restaurant?

A. Where's the restaurant?
B. It's **next to** the bank.

A. Where's the school?
B. It's **between** the library and the park.

A. Where's the supermarket?
B. It's **across** *the street* **from** the movie theater.

A. Where's the post office?
B. It's **around the corner from** the hospital.

---

1. Where's the bank?

2. Where's the post office?

3. Where's the restaurant?

4. Where's the hospital?
*Around the corner from the* hospital

5. Where's the hotel?

6. Where's the gas station?

7. Where's the clinic?

8. Where's the bakery?
*The barber shop is next to the bakery down the street from the video store*

# Is There a Laundromat in This Neighborhood?

| There's (There is) a bank on Main Street. |
| Is there a bank on Main Street? |

**A.** Excuse me. Is there a laundromat in this neighborhood?

**B.** Yes. There's a laundromat on Main Street, next to the supermarket.

**1.** *drug store?*

**2.** *clinic?*

**3.** *department store?*

**4.** *hair salon?*

**5.** *book store?*

**6.** *post office?*

## How to Say It!

### Expressing Gratitude

**A.** Thank you./Thanks.

**B.** You're welcome.

Practice some conversations on this page again.
Express gratitude at the end of each conversation.

| Is there . . . ? | Yes, there is.<br>No, there isn't. |

Is there a restaurant in your neighborhood?

No, there isn't.

Is there a cafeteria in your neighborhood?

Yes, there is.

Where is it?

It's on Central Avenue, across from the bank.

Draw a simple map of your neighborhood. With another student, ask and answer questions about your neighborhoods.

*Write sentences (5)*

**Some places you can talk about:**

| | | | |
|---|---|---|---|
| bakery | clinic | hospital | post office |
| bank | department store | hotel | restaurant |
| barber shop | drug store | laundromat | school |
| book store | fire station | library | supermarket |
| bus station | gas station | movie theater | train station |
| cafeteria | hair salon | park | video store |
| church | health club | police station | *train tracks* |

*supercalifragilisticexpialidocious*

*Mary Poppins*

# Is There a Stove in the Kitchen?

*bird     bid*

**A.** Is there a stove in the kitchen?

**B.** Yes, there is. There's a very nice stove in the kitchen.

**A.** Oh, good.

**A.** Is there a refrigerator in the kitchen?

**B.** No, there isn't.

**A.** Oh, I see.

*cabinete    cabinets*

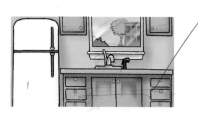

**1.** *a window in the kitchen?*
*Yes, . . .* It is on the wall over the sink.

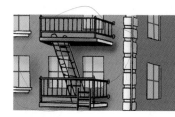

**2.** *a fire escape?*
*No, . . .*

**3.** *a closet in the bedroom?*
*Yes, . . .*

**4.** *an elevator\* in the building?*
*No, . . .*

**5.** *an air conditioner\* in the bedroom?*
*Yes, . . .*

**6.** *a superintendent in the building?*
*No, . . .*

**7.** *a bus stop near the building?*
*No, . . .*

**8.** *a jacuzzi in the bathroom?*
*Yes, . . .*     whirlpool bathtub

**a** stove        **an** elevator
**a** closet       **an** air conditioner

*cognate     Coke     Kleenex*

59

# How Many Bedrooms Are There in the Apartment?

How many windows **are there** in the bedroom? | **There's** one window in the bedroom.
**There are** two windows in the bedroom.

**A.** Tell me, how many bedrooms are there in the apartment?

**B.** There are two bedrooms in the apartment.

**A.** Two bedrooms?

**B.** Yes. That's right.

**1.** *floors*
*building*

**2.** *windows*
*living room*

**3.** *closets*
*apartment*

**4.** *apartments*
*building*

**5.** *washing machines*
*basement*

**6.** *bathrooms*
*apartment*

\* two and a half

# ROLE PLAY  *Looking for an Apartment*

| | |
|---|---|
| Is there a window?<br>Yes, there is. / No, there isn't. | Are there any windows?<br>Yes, there are. / No, there aren't. |

You're looking for a new apartment.  Practice with another student.  Ask questions about the apartment on page 61.

**Ask the landlord:**

1.  a stove in the kitchen?
2.  a refrigerator in the kitchen?
3.  a superintendent in the building?
4.  an elevator in the building?
5.  a fire escape?
6.  a satellite dish on the roof?
7.  a mailbox near the building?
8.  a bus stop near the building?

**Ask a tenant in the building:**

9.  children in the building?
10.  cats in the building?
11.  mice in the basement?
12.  cockroaches in the building?
13.  broken windows in the building?
14.  holes in the walls?
15.  washing machines in the basement?

**Ask the landlord:**

16.  rooms—in the apartment?
17.  floors—in the building?
18.  closets—in the bedroom?
19.  windows—in the living room?

*rat*
*rate*

*brew*
*rule of silent e*

*11/21*

## THE NEW SHOPPING MALL

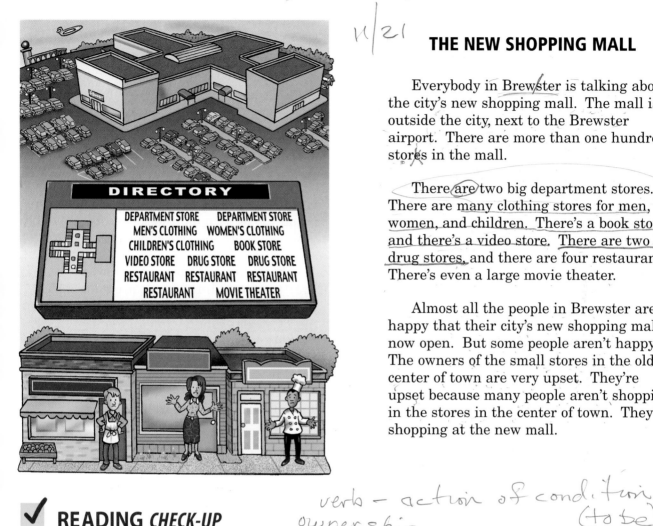

Everybody in Brewster is talking about the city's new shopping mall. The mall is outside the city, next to the Brewster airport. There are more than one hundred stores in the mall.

There are two big department stores. There are many clothing stores for men, women, and children. There's a book store, and there's a video store. There are two drug stores, and there are four restaurants. There's even a large movie theater.

Almost all the people in Brewster are happy that their city's new shopping mall is now open. But some people aren't happy. The owners of the small stores in the old center of town are very upset. They're upset because many people aren't shopping in the stores in the center of town. They're shopping at the new mall.

✔ **READING** *CHECK-UP*

*verb – action of condition*
*ownership* *(to be)*
*owner*
*owning*

### CHOOSE

1. Everybody in Brewster is ~~b~~ .
   a. at the airport
   b. outside the city
   c. talking about the mall

2. In the mall, there are **b** .
   a. two video stores
   b. two drug stores
   c. two restaurants

3. In the mall, there are **c** .
   a. book stores and cafeterias
   b. restaurants and drug stores
   c. clothing stores and video stores

4. The store owners in the center of town are upset because **a** .
   a. people aren't shopping in their stores
   b. people aren't shopping at the mall
   c. they're very old

## How About You?

Is there a shopping mall in your city or town?
Are there small stores in your city or town?
Tell about stores where you live.

## AMY'S APARTMENT BUILDING

Amy's apartment building is in the center of town. Amy is very happy there because the building is in a very convenient place.

Across from the building, there's a bank, a post office, and a restaurant. Next to the building, there's a drug store and a laundromat. Around the corner from the building, there are two supermarkets.

There's a lot of noise near Amy's apartment building. There are a lot of cars on the street, and there are a lot of people on the sidewalks all day and all night.

However, Amy isn't very upset about the noise in her neighborhood. Her building is in the center of town. It's a very busy place, but it's a convenient place to live.

## ✔ READING CHECK-UP

### WHAT'S THE ANSWER?

1. Where is Amy's apartment building?
2. What's across from her building?
3. Is there a laundromat near her building?
4. Why is there a lot of noise near Amy's building?
5. Why is Amy happy there?

### TRUE OR FALSE?

T 1. Amy's apartment is in a convenient place.
F 2. There's a drug store around the corner from her building.
F 3. There are two supermarkets in her neighborhood.
F 4. There are a lot of cars on the sidewalk.
F 5. The center of town is very noisy.

**How About You?**

Tell about YOUR neighborhood.
Is it convenient? Is it very busy?
Is it noisy or quiet?

# IN YOUR OWN WORDS

### FOR WRITING AND DISCUSSION

*5-story building*

*4/5*

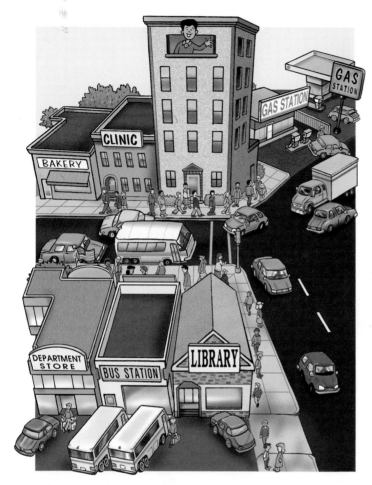

## EDWARD'S APARTMENT BUILDING

Edward's apartment building is in the center of town. Edward is very happy there because the building is in a very convenient place. Using this picture, tell about Edward's neighborhood.

# LISTENING

### WHAT PLACES DO YOU HEAR?

Listen and choose the correct places.

| | | | |
|---|---|---|---|
| *Example:* | (a.) supermarket | b. school | (c.) video store |
| **1.** | a. park | b. bank | c. laundromat |
| **2.** | a. fire station | b. police station | c. gas station |
| **3.** | a. school | b. department store | c. clothing store |
| **4.** | a. bank | b. drug store | c. book store |
| **5.** | a. hotel | b. hair salon | c. hospital |

### TRUE OR FALSE?

Listen to the conversation. Then answer *True* or *False*.

1. There are four rooms in the apartment.
2. There are two closets in the bedroom.
3. There are four windows in the kitchen.
4. There's a superintendent in the building.
5. There are three washing machines.
6. There's an elevator in the building.

# PRONUNCIATION  *Rising Intonation to Check Understanding*

**Listen.  Then say it.**

Two bedrooms?

Five closets?

Next to the bank?

On Main Street?

**Say it.  Then listen.**

Three windows?

Twenty floors?

Across from the clinic?

On Central Avenue?

In your journal, write about your apartment building or home.  Tell about the building and the neighborhood.

# CHAPTER SUMMARY

## GRAMMAR

### THERE IS/THERE ARE

There's one window in the bedroom.

Is there a laundromat in this neighborhood?
Yes, there is.
No, there isn't.

There are two windows in the bedroom.

Are there any children in the building?
Yes, there are.
No, there aren't.

### PREPOSITIONS

It's next to the bank.
It's across from the movie theater.
It's between the library and the park.
It's around the corner from the hospital.

### SINGULAR/PLURAL: INTRODUCTION

There's one bedroom in the apartment.
There are two bedrooms in the apartment.

## KEY VOCABULARY

### PLACES AROUND TOWN

| | | |
|---|---|---|
| airport | drug store | police station |
| bakery | fire station | post office |
| bank | gas station | restaurant |
| barber shop | hair salon | school |
| book store | health club | shopping mall |
| bus station | hospital | supermarket |
| cafeteria | hotel | train station |
| church | laundromat | video store |
| clinic | library | zoo |
| clothing store | movie theater | |
| department store | park | |

### HOUSING

| | |
|---|---|
| air conditioner | floor |
| apartment building | jacuzzi |
| building | mailbox |
| bus stop | refrigerator |
| closet | stove |
| elevator | superintendent |
| fire escape | washing machine |

# 8

## Singular/Plural
## Adjectives
## This/That/These/Those

- **Clothing**
- **Colors**
- **Shopping for Clothing**

### VOCABULARY PREVIEW

1. shirt
2. coat
3. dress
4. skirt
5. blouse
6. jacket
7. suit
8. tie
9. belt
10. sweater
11. pants
12. jeans
13. pajamas
14. shoes
15. socks

'cot
cat
ti
fe
scat
sit

When 2 vowels go walking
the first one does the talking.

# Clothing

| | | | |
|---|---|---|---|
| **1.** shirt | **8.** earring | **15.** hat | **21.** suit |
| **2.** tie | **9.** necklace | **16.** coat | **22.** watch |
| **3.** jacket | **10.** blouse | **17.** glove | **23.** umbrella |
| **4.** belt | **11.** bracelet | **18.** purse / | **24.** sweater |
| **5.** pants | **12.** skirt | pocketbook | **25.** mitten |
| **6.** sock | **13.** briefcase | **19.** dress | **26.** jeans |
| **7.** shoe | **14.** stocking | **20.** glasses | **27.** boot |

# Shirts Are Over There

| s | z | iz |
|---|---|---|
| a shirt – shirts | a tie – ties | a dress – dresses |
| a coat – coats | an umbrella – umbrellas | a watch – watches |
| a hat – hats | a sweater – sweaters | a blouse – blouses |
| a belt – belts | | a necklace – necklaces |

**A.** Excuse me.
I'm looking for **a shirt**.

**B.** **Shirts** are over there.

**A.** Thanks.

**A.** Excuse me.
I'm looking for **a tie**.

**B.** **Ties** are over there.

**A.** Thanks.

**A.** Excuse me.
I'm looking for **a dress**.

**B.** **Dresses** are over there.

**A.** Thanks.

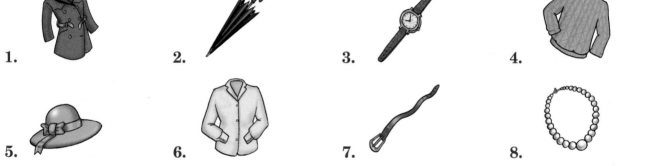

1.
2.
3.
4.
5.
6.
7.
8.

**Put these words in the correct column.**

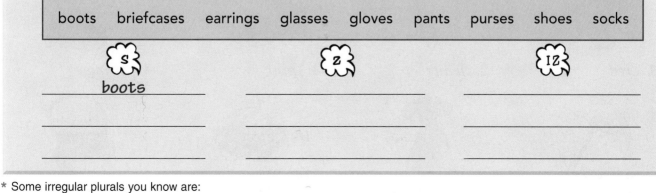

boots    briefcases    earrings    glasses    gloves    pants    purses    shoes    socks

| s | z | iz |
|---|---|---|
| boots | | |
| | | |
| | | |

* Some irregular plurals you know are:

a man – men          a child – children          a tooth – teeth
a woman – women      a person – people           a mouse – mice

# I'm Looking for a Jacket

## COLORS

red   orange   yellow   green   blue   purple   black   silver

pink   gray   white   gold   brown

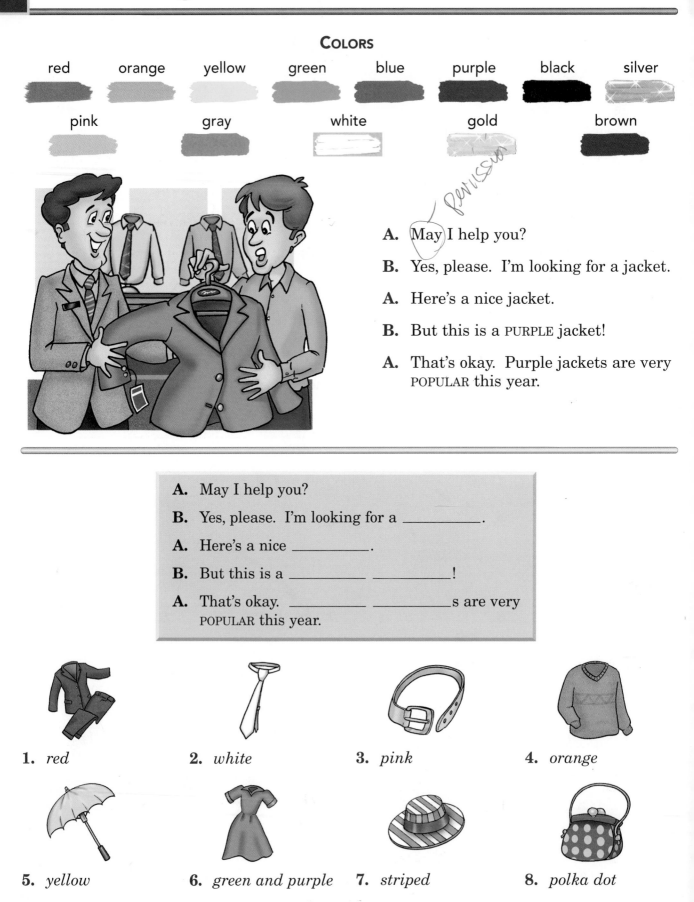

**A.** May I help you?

**B.** Yes, please. I'm looking for a jacket.

**A.** Here's a nice jacket.

**B.** But this is a PURPLE jacket!

**A.** That's okay. Purple jackets are very POPULAR this year.

---

**A.** May I help you?

**B.** Yes, please. I'm looking for a _____.

**A.** Here's a nice _____.

**B.** But this is a _____ _____!

**A.** That's okay. _____ _____s are very POPULAR this year.

1. *red*

2. *white*

3. *pink*

4. *orange*

5. *yellow*

6. *green and purple*

7. *striped*

8. *polka dot*

# I'm Looking for a Pair of Gloves

*homophone*

*pair - pear*

pair of shoes/socks . . .

*may — Ability*

**A.** Can I help you?

**B.** Yes, please. I'm looking for a pair of gloves.

**A.** Here's a nice pair of gloves.

**B.** But these are GREEN gloves!

**A.** That's okay. Green gloves are very POPULAR this year.

---

*may*

*to two too*

**A.** Can I help you?

**B.** Yes, please. I'm looking for a pair of _____.

**A.** Here's a nice pair of _____.

**B.** But these are _____ _____s!

**A.** That's okay. _____ _____s are very POPULAR this year.

**1.** *yellow*

**2.** *blue*

**3.** *pink*

**4.** *orange*

**5.** *striped*

**6.** *green*

**7.** *red, white, and blue*

**8.** *polka dot*

## How About You?

What are you wearing today?
What are the students in your class wearing today?
What's your favorite color?

## NOTHING TO WEAR

Fred is upset this morning. He's looking for something to wear to work, but there's nothing in his closet.

He's looking for a clean shirt, but all his shirts are dirty. He's looking for a sports jacket, but all his sports jackets are at the dry cleaner's. He's looking for a pair of pants, but all the pants in his closet are ripped. And he's looking for a pair of socks, but all his socks are on the clothesline, and it's raining!

Fred is having a difficult time this morning. He's getting dressed for work, but his closet is empty, and there's nothing to wear.

## ✔ READING CHECK-UP

### CHOOSE

1. Fred's closet is _____.
   a. upset
   b. empty

2. Fred is _____.
   a. at home
   b. at work

3. Fred's shirts are _____.
   a. dirty
   b. clean

4. He's looking for a pair of _____.
   a. jackets
   b. pants

5. The weather is _____.
   a. not very good
   b. beautiful

6. Fred is upset because _____.
   a. he's getting dressed
   b. there's nothing to wear

### WHICH WORD DOESN'T BELONG?

|  | a. | b. | c. | d. |
|---|---|---|---|---|
| *Example:* | socks | stockings | jeans | shoes |
| 1. | sweater | jacket | briefcase | coat |
| 2. | necklace | belt | bracelet | earrings |
| 3. | blouse | skirt | dress | tie |
| 4. | clean | green | gray | blue |
| 5. | pants | shoes | earrings | blouse |

# Excuse Me. I Think That's My Jacket.

This / That is     These / Those are

1. hat
2. boots
3. coat
4. pen
5. pencils
6. umbrella
7. sunglasses
8.

# Lost and Found

A. Is this your umbrella?

B. No, it isn't.

A. Are you sure?

B. Yes. THAT umbrella is BROWN, and MY umbrella is BLACK.

A. Are these your boots?

B. No, they aren't.

A. Are you sure?

B. Yes. THOSE boots are DIRTY, and MY boots are CLEAN.

---

**Make up conversations, using colors and other adjectives you know.**

1. *watch*  2. *gloves*  3. *briefcase*  4. *mittens*  5. _____

---

## How to Say It!

**Complimenting**

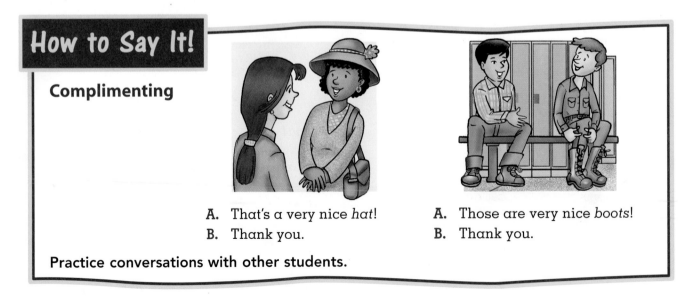

A. That's a very nice *hat*!
B. Thank you.

A. Those are very nice *boots*!
B. Thank you.

**Practice conversations with other students.**

# READING

## HOLIDAY SHOPPING

Mrs. Miller is doing her holiday shopping. She's looking for gifts for her family, but she's having a lot of trouble.

She's looking for a brown umbrella for her son, but all the umbrellas are black. She's looking for a gray raincoat for her daughter, but all the raincoats are yellow. She's looking for a cotton sweater for her husband, but all the sweaters are wool.

She's looking for an inexpensive bracelet for her sister, but all the bracelets are expensive. She's looking for a leather purse for her mother, but all the purses are vinyl. And she's looking for a polka dot tie for her father, but all the ties are striped.

Poor Mrs. Miller is very frustrated. She's looking for special gifts for all the special people in her family, but she's having a lot of trouble.

## ✔ READING *CHECK-UP*

### Q & A

Mrs. Miller is in the department store. Using this model, create dialogs based on the story.

**A.** Excuse me. I'm looking for *a brown umbrella* for my *son.*
**B.** I'm sorry. All our *umbrellas* are *black.*

# LISTENING

## WHAT'S THE WORD?

Listen and choose the correct answer.

1. a. blouse       b. dress
2. a. shoes        b. boots
3. a. necklace     b. bracelet
4. a. coat         b. raincoat
5. a. socks        b. stockings
6. a. shirt        b. skirt

## WHICH WORD DO YOU HEAR?

Listen and choose the correct answer.

1. a. jacket       b. jackets
2. a. belt         b. belts
3. a. sweater      b. sweaters
4. a. suit         b. suits
5. a. shoe         b. shoes
6. a. tie          b. ties

75

## PRONUNCIATION *Emphasized Words*

**Listen. Then say it.**

But this is a PURPLE jacket!

Green gloves are very POPULAR this year.

I think this is MY jacket.

THAT umbrella is BROWN, and
    MY umbrella is BLACK.

**Say it. Then listen.**

But these are YELLOW shoes!

Striped socks are very POPULAR this year.

I think these are MY glasses.

THOSE boots are DIRTY, and
    MY boots are CLEAN.

SIDE by SIDE JOURNAL

What are you wearing today? Tell about the clothing and the colors. Write about it in your journal.

---

# CHAPTER SUMMARY

## GRAMMAR

### SINGULAR/PLURAL

[s]   I'm looking for **a** coat.
Coat**s** are over there.

[z]   I'm looking for **an** umbrella.
Umbrella**s** are over there.

[ɪz]   I'm looking for **a** dress.
Dress**es** are over there.

### THIS/THAT/THESE/THOSE

Is **this** your umbrella?
**That** umbrella is brown.

Are **these** your boots?
**Those** boots are dirty.

### ADJECTIVES

This is a **purple** jacket.
These are **green** gloves.

## KEY VOCABULARY

### CLOTHING

| | | |
|---|---|---|
| belt | jacket | skirt |
| blouse | jeans | sock |
| boots | mittens | sports jacket |
| bracelet | necklace | stocking |
| briefcase | pajamas | suit |
| coat | pants | sunglasses |
| dress | pocketbook | sweater |
| earring | purse | tie |
| glasses | raincoat | umbrella |
| glove | shirt | watch |
| hat | shoe | |

### COLORS

| | |
|---|---|
| black | pink |
| blue | purple |
| brown | red |
| gold | silver |
| gray | white |
| green | yellow |
| orange | |

# Clothing, Colors, and Cultures

**Blue and pink aren't children's clothing colors all around the world**

The meanings of colors are sometimes very different in different cultures. For example, in some cultures, blue is a common clothing color for little boys, and pink is a common clothing color for little girls. In other cultures, other colors are <u>common</u> for boys and girls.

There are also different colors for special days in different cultures. For example, white is the traditional color of a wedding dress in some cultures, but other colors are traditional in other cultures.

For some people, white is a happy color. For others, it's a <u>sad</u> color. For some people, red is a beautiful and lucky color. For others, it's a very sad color.

*What are the meanings of different colors in* YOUR *culture?*

## LISTENING

### Attention, J-Mart Shoppers!

| | | |
|---|---|---|
| _c_ ① jackets | **a.** | Aisle 1 |
| ____ ② gloves | **b.** | Aisle 7 |
| ____ ③ blouses | **c.** | Aisle 9 |
| ____ ④ bracelets | **d.** | Aisle 11 |
| ____ ⑤ ties | **e.** | Aisle 5 |

## BUILD YOUR VOCABULARY!
### Clothing

**That's a very nice _____ .**

- bathrobe
- tee shirt
- scarf
- wallet
- ring

**Those are very nice _____ .**

- sandals
- slippers
- sneakers
- shorts
- sweat pants

## People's Homes

**H**omes are different all around the world.

This family is living in a farmhouse.

This family is living in a hut.

This family is living in a houseboat.

These people are living in a mobile home (a trailer).

**What different kinds of homes are there in your country?**

## FACT FILE

### Urban, Suburban, and Rural

| | | |
|---|---|---|
| **urban** areas | = | cities |
| **suburban** areas | = | places near cities |
| **rural** areas | = | places in the countryside, far from cities |

About 50% (percent) of the world's population is in urban and suburban areas.

About 50% (percent) of the world's population is in rural areas.

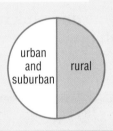

## Global Exchange

**RosieM:** My apartment is in a wonderful neighborhood. There's a big, beautiful park across from my apartment building. Around the corner, there's a bank, a post office, and a laundromat. There are also many restaurants and stores in my neighborhood. It's a noisy place, but it's a very interesting place. There are a lot of people on the sidewalks all day and all night. How about your neighborhood? Tell me about it.

**Send a message to a keypal. Tell about your neighborhood.**

## What Are They Saying?

# 9

## Simple Present Tense

- **Languages and Nationalities**
- **Everyday Activities**

### VOCABULARY PREVIEW

1. call
2. cook
3. drive
4. eat
5. listen to music
6. paint
7. play
8. read
9. sell
10. shop
11. sing
12. speak
13. visit
14. watch TV
15. work

# Interviews Around the World

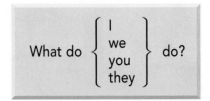

$\left.\begin{array}{l}\text{I} \\ \text{We} \\ \text{You} \\ \text{They}\end{array}\right\}$ live.

Where do $\left.\begin{array}{l}\text{I} \\ \text{we} \\ \text{you} \\ \text{they}\end{array}\right\}$ live?

What do $\left.\begin{array}{l}\text{I} \\ \text{we} \\ \text{you} \\ \text{they}\end{array}\right\}$ do?

**A.** What's your name?

**B.** My name is Antonio.

**A.** Where do you live?

**B.** I live in Rome.

**A.** What language do you speak?

**B.** I speak Italian.

**A.** Tell me, what do you do every day?

**B.** I eat Italian food,
I sing Italian songs,
and I watch Italian TV shows!

**Interview these people.**

What's your name?
Where do you live?
What language do you speak?
What do you do every day?

1. Carmen — Spanish — MADRID

2. Kenji — Japanese — TOKYO

3. Nicole — French — PARIS

4. Erik and Monika — German — BERLIN

5. Jae Hee — Korean — SEOUL

6. Boris and Natasha — Russian — MOSCOW

# People Around the World

| He<br>She<br>It } lives. | Where <u>does</u> { he<br>she<br>it } live? | What does { he<br>she<br>it } do? |
|---|---|---|

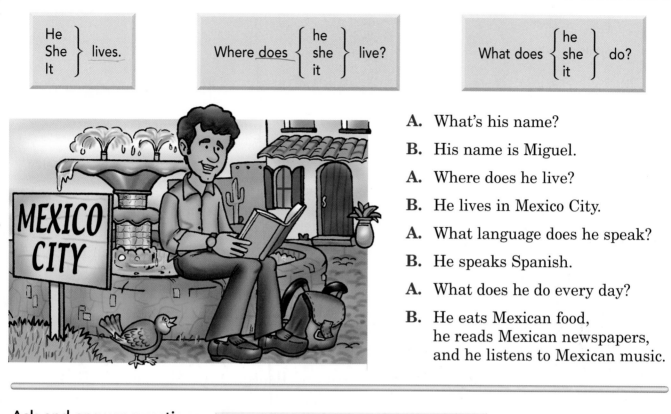

A. What's his name?

B. His name is Miguel.

A. Where does he live?

B. He lives in Mexico City.

A. What language does he speak?

B. He speaks Spanish.

A. What does he do every day?

B. He eats Mexican food,
he reads Mexican newspapers,
and he listens to Mexican music.

**Ask and answer questions about these people.**

> What's his/her name?
> Where does he/she live?
> What language does he/she speak?
> What does he/she do every day?

1. Kate — English / Canadian — TORONTO

2. Carlos — Spanish / Puerto Rican — SAN JUAN

3. Anna — Greek — ATHENS

4. Ming — Chinese — HONG KONG

5. Sonia — Portuguese / Brazilian — RIO de JANEIRO

6. Omar — Arabic / Egyptian — CAIRO

# TALK ABOUT IT! *Where Do They Live, and What Do They Do?*

Use these models to talk with other students about the people above.

**A.** Where does *Linda* live?

**B.** *She* lives in *London*.

**A.** What does *she* do?

**B.** *She works in a library*.

**A.** Where do *Walter* and *Wendy* live?

**B.** They live in *Washington, D.C.*

**A.** What do they do?

**B.** They *work in an office*.

**How About You?**

Where do you live?
What do you do?

## MR. AND MRS. DiCARLO

Mr. and Mrs. DiCarlo live in an old Italian neighborhood in New York City. They speak a little English, but usually they speak Italian.

They read the Italian newspaper. They listen to Italian radio programs. They shop at the Italian grocery store around the corner from their apartment building. And every day they visit their friends and neighbors and talk about life back in "the old country."

Mr. and Mrs. DiCarlo are upset about their son, Joe. He lives in a small suburb outside the city. He speaks a little Italian, but usually he speaks English. He reads American newspapers. He listens to American radio programs. He shops at big suburban supermarkets and shopping malls. And when he visits his friends and neighbors, he always speaks English.

In fact, Joe speaks Italian only when he calls his parents on the telephone, or when he visits them every weekend.

Mr. and Mrs. DiCarlo are sad because their son speaks so little Italian. They're afraid he's forgetting his language, his culture, and his country.

## ✔ READING CHECK-UP

### WHAT'S THE ANSWER?

1. Where do Mr. and Mrs. DiCarlo live?
2. Where does Joe live?
3. What language do Mr. and Mrs. DiCarlo usually speak?
4. What language does Joe usually speak?
5. What do Mr. and Mrs. DiCarlo read?
6. What does Joe read?
7. What do Mr. and Mrs. DiCarlo listen to?
8. What does Joe listen to?
9. Where do Mr. and Mrs. DiCarlo shop?
10. Where does Joe shop?

### WHICH WORD IS CORRECT?

1. Mrs. DiCarlo ( read  reads ) the Italian newspaper.
2. Mr. DiCarlo ( shop  shops ) at the Italian grocery store.
3. They ( live  lives ) in New York City.
4. Joe ( live  lives ) outside the city.
5. He ( speak  speaks ) English.
6. Mr. and Mrs. DiCarlo ( listen  listens ) to the radio.
7. They ( visit  visits ) their friends every day.
8. Their friends ( talk  talks ) about life back in "the old country."
9. Joe ( call  calls ) his parents on the telephone.
10. Joe's friends ( speak  speaks ) English.

## LISTENING

**Listen and choose the correct answer.**

1. a. live        b. lives
2. a. work        b. works
3. a. speak       b. speaks
4. a. drive       b. drives
5. a. read        b. reads
6. a. visit       b. visits
7. a. cook        b. cooks
8. a. paint       b. paints
9. a. call        b. calls
10. a. shop       b. shops

## How to Say It!

### Hesitating

A. What do you do every day?
B. Hmm. Well . . .
   I *work*, I *read the newspaper*, and I *visit my friends*.

**Practice conversations with other students. Hesitate while you're thinking of your answer.**

# IN YOUR OWN WORDS

## MRS. KOWALSKI

Mrs. Kowalski lives in an old Polish neighborhood in Chicago. She's upset about her son, Michael, and his wife, Kathy. Using the story on page 83 as a model, tell a story about Mrs. Kowalski.

# INTERVIEW

> Where do you live?
> What language do you speak?
> What do you do every day?

Interview another student.

Then tell the class about that person.

I live in an apartment in the city.
I speak Spanish and a little English.
I go to school and visit my friends.

She lives in an apartment in the city.
She speaks Spanish and a little English.
She goes to school and visits her friends.

## PRONUNCIATION  Blending with *does*

**Listen.  Then say it.**

Where does he work?

Where does she live?

What does he do?

What does she read?

**Say it.  Then listen.**

Where does he shop?

Where does she eat?

What does he cook?

What does she talk about?

Where do you live?  What language do you speak?  What do you do every day?  Write a paragraph about it in your journal.

## CHAPTER SUMMARY

### GRAMMAR

**SIMPLE PRESENT TENSE**

| Where | do | I we you they | live? |
|---|---|---|---|
| | does | he she it | |

| I We You They | live | in Rome. |
|---|---|---|
| He She It | lives | |

### KEY VOCABULARY

**EVERYDAY ACTIVITIES**

| | |
|---|---|
| call | sell |
| cook | shop |
| drive | sing |
| eat | speak |
| listen | visit |
| paint | watch TV |
| play | work |
| read | |

**NATIONALITIES**

Brazilian
Canadian
Chinese
Egyptian
French
German
Greek
Italian

**LANGUAGES**

Portuguese
English, French
Chinese
Arabic
French
German
Greek
Italian

**NATIONALITIES**

Japanese
Korean
Mexican
Polish
Puerto Rican
Russian
Spanish

**LANGUAGES**

Japanese
Korean
Spanish
Polish
Spanish
Russian
Spanish

# Simple Present Tense:
# Yes/No Questions
# Negatives
# Short Answers

10

- **Habitual Actions**
- **People's Interests and Activities**

## VOCABULARY PREVIEW

1. Sunday
2. Monday
3. Tuesday
4. Wednesday
5. Thursday
6. Friday
7. Saturday

8. baby-sit
9. clean
10. do yoga
11. go dancing
12. jog

13. play volleyball
14. ride
15. see a movie
16. see a play

87

# Stanley's International Restaurant

He cooks.
He doesn't cook.
(does not)

Does he cook?
Yes, he does.
No, he doesn't.

What kind of food
When } does he cook?

| MONDAY | TUESDAY | WEDNESDAY | THURSDAY | FRIDAY | SATURDAY | SUNDAY |
|--------|---------|-----------|----------|--------|----------|--------|
| Italian | Greek | Chinese | Puerto Rican | Japanese | Mexican | American |

Stanley's International Restaurant is a very special place. Every day Stanley cooks a different kind of food. On Monday he cooks Italian food. On Tuesday he cooks Greek food. On Wednesday he cooks Chinese food. On Thursday he cooks Puerto Rican food. On Friday he cooks Japanese food. On Saturday he cooks Mexican food. And on Sunday he cooks American food.

**A.** What kind of food does Stanley cook on **Monday**?

**B.** On **Monday** he cooks **Italian** food.

**Ask and answer questions about the other days of the week.**

**A.** Does Stanley cook **Greek** food on **Tuesday**?

**B.** Yes, he does.

**Ask six questions with "yes" answers.**

**A.** Does Stanley cook **Japanese** food on **Sunday**?

**B.** No, he doesn't.

**A.** When does he cook **Japanese** food?

**B.** He cooks **Japanese** food on **Friday**.

**Ask six questions with "no" answers.**

| You go. You don't go. (do not) | Do you go? Yes, I do. / Yes, we do. No, I don't. / No, we don't. | When do you go? |
|---|---|---|

**A.** Do you go to Stanley's Restaurant on **Wednesday**?

**B.** Yes, I do.

**A.** Why?

**B.** Because I like **Chinese** food.

**Ask these people.**

1. *Monday?*     2. *Thursday?*     3. *Saturday?*     4. *Sunday?*

---

**A.** Do you go to Stanley's Restaurant on **Sunday**?

**B.** No, I don't.

**A.** Why not?

**B.** Because I don't like **American** food.

**Ask these people.**

5. *Tuesday?*     6. *Wednesday?*     7. *Friday?*     8. *Monday?*

---

**A.** What kind of food do you like?

**B.** I like **Russian** food.

**A.** When do you go to Stanley's Restaurant?

**B.** I don't go there.

**A.** Why not?

**B.** Because Stanley doesn't cook **Russian** food.

**Ask these people.**

9. *French*     10. *Ethiopian*     11. *Thai*     12. *Vietnamese*

# Busy People!

Jeff is a very athletic person. He does a different kind of exercise or sport every day. On Monday he jogs. On Tuesday he plays tennis. On Wednesday he does yoga. On Thursday he swims. On Friday he goes to a health club. On Saturday he plays basketball. And on Sunday he rides his bike.

Julie is a very busy student. She does a different activity every day. On Monday she sings in the choir. On Tuesday she plays in the orchestra. On Wednesday she writes for the school newspaper. On Thursday she plays volleyball. On Friday she baby-sits for her neighbors. On Saturday she works at the mall. And on Sunday she visits her grandparents.

Mr. and Mrs. Baker are very active people. They do something different every day of the week. On Monday they go to a museum. On Tuesday they see a play. On Wednesday they go to a concert. On Thursday they take a karate lesson. On Friday they go dancing. On Saturday they see a movie. And on Sunday they play cards with their friends.

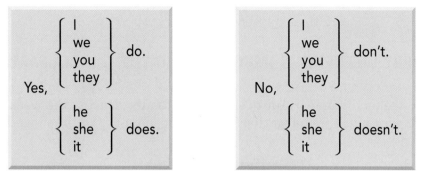

**A.** Does Jeff play tennis on Tuesday?

**B.** Yes, he does.

**A.** Does Julie work at the mall on Saturday?

**B.** Yes, she does.

**A.** Do Mr. and Mrs. Baker go dancing on Friday?

**B.** Yes, they do.

**Ask other questions with "yes" answers.**

**A.** Does Jeff do yoga on Sunday?

**B.** No, he doesn't.

**A.** Does Julie sing in the choir on Thursday?

**B.** No, she doesn't.

**A.** Do Mr. and Mrs. Baker see a movie on Monday?

**B.** No, they don't.

**Ask other questions with "no" answers.**

**Now interview Jeff, Julie, and Mr. and Mrs. Baker. Practice conversations with other students.**

91

## EVERY WEEKEND IS IMPORTANT TO THE GARCIA FAMILY

Every weekend is important to the Garcia family. During the week they don't have very much time together, but they spend a LOT of time together on the weekend.

Mr. Garcia works at the post office during the week, but he doesn't work there on the weekend. Mrs. Garcia works at the bank during the week, but she doesn't work there on the weekend. Jennifer and Jonathan Garcia go to school during the week, but they don't go to school on the weekend. And the Garcias' dog, Max, stays home alone during the week, but he doesn't stay home alone on the weekend.

On Saturday and Sunday the Garcias spend time together. On Saturday morning they clean the house together. On Saturday afternoon they work in the garden together. And on Saturday evening they watch videos together. On Sunday morning they go to church together. On Sunday afternoon they have a big dinner together. And on Sunday evening they play their musical instruments together.

As you can see, every weekend is special to the Garcias. It's their only time together as a family.

# ✔ READING CHECK-UP

## Q & A

**Using these models, make questions and answers based on the story on page 92.**

A. What *does Mr. Garcia* do during the week?
B. *He works at the post office.*

A. What do the Garcias do on *Saturday morning*?
B. They *clean the house* together.

## Do or Does?

1. _____ Mr. Garcia work on the weekend?
2. _____ Jennifer and Jonathan go to school during the week?
3. When _____ they watch videos?
4. Where _____ Mrs. Garcia work?
5. _____ you speak Spanish?
6. What _____ Mr. Garcia do during the week?

## What's the Answer?

1. Does Mr. Garcia work at the post office?
2. Do Jennifer and Jonathan go to school during the week?
3. Does Mrs. Garcia work at the post office?
4. Do Mr. and Mrs. Garcia have much time together during the week?
5. Does Jennifer watch videos on Saturday evening?
6. Do Jennifer and her brother clean the house on Saturday morning?
7. Does Mr. Garcia work in the garden on Saturday evening?

## Don't or Doesn't?

1. Mr. and Mrs. Garcia _____ work on the weekend.
2. Jennifer _____ work at the bank.
3. We _____ watch videos during the week.
4. My son _____ play a musical instrument.
5. My sister and I _____ eat at Stanley's Restaurant.
6. Our dog _____ like our neighbor's dog.

# LISTENING

## What's the Word?

**Listen and choose the word you hear.**

1. a. do          b. does
2. a. do          b. does
3. a. Sunday      b. Monday
4. a. don't       b. doesn't
5. a. don't       b. doesn't
6. a. does        b. goes
7. a. Tuesday     b. Thursday
8. a. go          b. don't

## What's the Answer?

**Listen and choose the correct response.**

1. a. Yes, I do.          b. Yes, he does.
2. a. Yes, they do.       b. Yes, she does.
3. a. No, she doesn't.    b. No, we don't.
4. a. No, he doesn't.     b. No, we don't.
5. a. No, I don't.        b. No, he doesn't.
6. a. No, I don't.        b. No, they don't.
7. a. Yes, we do.         b. Yes, they do.
8. a. Yes, they do.       b. Yes, he does.

## How About You?

Tell about yourself:
What do you do during the week?
What do you do on the weekend?

Now tell about another person—a friend, someone in your family, or another student:
What does he/she do during the week?
What does he/she do on the weekend?

## READING

### A VERY OUTGOING PERSON

Alice is a very outgoing person. She spends a lot of time with her friends. She goes to parties, she goes to movies, and she goes to concerts. She's very popular.

She also likes sports very much. She plays basketball, she plays baseball, and she plays volleyball. She's very athletic.

Alice doesn't stay home alone very often. She doesn't read many books, she doesn't watch TV, and she doesn't listen to music. She's very active.

As you can see, Alice is a very outgoing person.

## IN YOUR OWN WORDS

### For Writing and Discussion

### A VERY SHY PERSON

Using the story about Alice as a model, tell a story about Sheldon. Begin your story:

Sheldon is a very shy person. He doesn't spend a lot of time with his friends. He doesn't go . . .

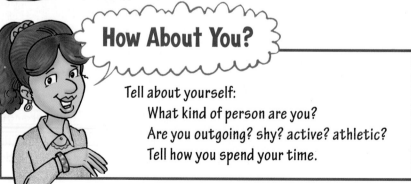

### How About You?

Tell about yourself:
  What kind of person are you?
  Are you outgoing? shy? active? athletic?
  Tell how you spend your time.

## How to Say It!

### Starting a Conversation

A. Tell me, what kind of *movies* do you like?
B. I like *comedies*.
A. Who's your favorite *movie star*?
B. *Tim Kelly*.

**Practice the interviews on this page, using "Tell me" to start the conversations.**

# INTERVIEW

First, answer these questions about yourself. Next, interview another student.
Then, tell the class about yourself and the other student.

1. What kind of movies do you like?

   Who's your favorite movie star?

   comedies    dramas    westerns    adventure movies    science fiction movies    cartoons

2. What kind of books do you like?

   Who's your favorite author?

   novels    poetry    short stories    non-fiction    biographies

3. What kind of TV programs do you like?

   Who's your favorite TV star?

     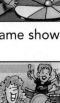  

   comedies    dramas    cartoons    game shows    news programs

4. What kind of music do you like?

   Who's your favorite performer?

   classical music    popular music    jazz    rock music    country music

5. What kind of sports do you like?

   Who's your favorite athlete? What's your favorite team?

   football    baseball    soccer    golf    hockey    tennis

95

**Listen. Then say it.**

What kind of movies do you like?

What kind of books do you like?

She spends a lot of time with her friends.

**Say it. Then listen.**

What kind of music do you like?

What kind of TV programs do you like?

I read a lot of books.

**SIDE by SIDE JOURNAL**

What do you do during the week? What do you do on the weekend? Write about it in your journal.

# CHAPTER SUMMARY

## GRAMMAR

### SIMPLE PRESENT TENSE: YES/NO QUESTIONS

| Do | I we you they | work? |
|---|---|---|
| Does | he she it | |

### SHORT ANSWERS

| Yes, | I we you they | do. |
|---|---|---|
| | he she it | does. |

| No, | I we you they | don't. |
|---|---|---|
| | he she it | doesn't. |

### SIMPLE PRESENT TENSE: NEGATIVES

| I We You They | don't | work. |
|---|---|---|
| He She It | doesn't | |

## KEY VOCABULARY

| DAYS OF THE WEEK | NATIONALITIES | LANGUAGES | DESCRIBING PEOPLE | EVERYDAY ACTIVITIES | |
|---|---|---|---|---|---|
| Sunday | American | English | active | baby-sit | play volleyball |
| Monday | Chinese | Chinese | athletic | clean | ride a bicycle |
| Tuesday | Greek | Greek | busy | do yoga | see a movie |
| Wednesday | Italian | Italian | outgoing | go dancing | see a play |
| Thursday | Japanese | Japanese | popular | jog | |
| Friday | Mexican | Spanish | shy | | |
| Saturday | Puerto Rican | Spanish | | | |

# Language

## Millions speak Chinese. Only hundreds speak Bahinemo.

There are over 20,000 languages in the world. Some of these languages are very common. For example, millions of people speak Chinese, Spanish, English, Arabic, Portuguese, and Japanese. On the other hand, some languages are very rare. For example, only 500 people in Papua, New Guinea speak the language Bahinemo.

Languages grow and change. They borrow words from other languages. For example, in the English language, the word *rodeo* is from Spanish, *cafe* comes from French, *ketchup* is from Chinese, *sofa* is from Arabic, and *potato* comes from Haitian Kreyol. New words also come from technology. For example, *cyberspace*, *website*, and *e-mail* are recent words that relate to the Internet.

## FACT FILE

### Common Languages

Mandarin Chinese    Hindi
Spanish    Portuguese
English    Russian
Arabic    Japanese
Bengali    German

| Language | Number of Speakers | Language | Number of Speakers |
|---|---|---|---|
| Mandarin Chinese | 885 million | Hindi | 182 million |
| Spanish | 332 million | Portuguese | 170 million |
| English | 322 million | Russian | 170 million |
| Arabic | 268 million | Japanese | 125 million |
| Bengali | 189 million | German | 98 million |

**BUILD YOUR VOCABULARY!**
Everyday Activities

Every day I _____ .

- get up
- take a shower
- brush my teeth
- comb my hair
- get dressed
- go to school
- go to work
- eat
- take a bath
- go to bed

## Exercising

**P**eople around the world exercise in different ways.

Some people exercise in health clubs.

Some people exercise at the beach.

Some people go hiking.

And some people exercise together outdoors.

How do people exercise in your country?

### Global Exchange

**Jogger9:** I'm a very active person. I jog and I swim. I go to a lot of movies and concerts. I sing in a choir. I play basketball with my friends every weekend. I like rock music and jazz. I don't watch TV very often. I only watch news programs. I read a lot of books. I like novels. My favorite author is Tom Clancy. How about you? Tell me about your activities and interests.

Send a message to a keypal. Tell about your activities and interests.

### LISTENING

*jazz* *poetry*

## Hello! This Is the International Cafe!

| | | | | |
|---|---|---|---|---|
| _c_ | **1** Monday | | **a.** | jazz |
| ___ | **2** Tuesday | | **b.** | rock music |
| ___ | **3** Wednesday | | **c.** | classical music |
| ___ | **4** Thursday | | **d.** | popular music |
| ___ | **5** Friday | | **e.** | poetry |
| ___ | **6** Saturday | | **f.** | country music |
| ___ | **7** Sunday | | **g.** | short stories |

### What Are They Saying?

# Object Pronouns
# Simple Present Tense: -s vs. non-s Endings
# Have/Has
# Adverbs of Frequency

- Describing Frequency of Actions
- Describing People

## VOCABULARY PREVIEW

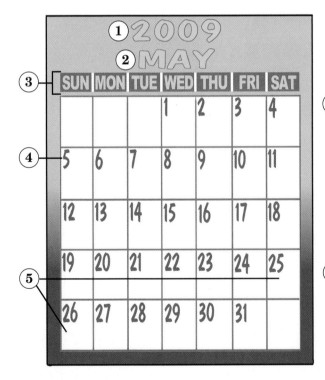

1. year
2. month
3. week
4. day
5. weekend

6. morning
7. afternoon
8. evening
9. night

# How Often?

| | |
|---|---|
| I | me |
| he | him |
| she | her |
| it | it |
| we | us |
| you | you |
| they | them |

**A.** How often does your boyfriend call you?

**B.** He calls me every night.

---

**1.** How often do you use
your computer?
*every day*

**2.** How often do you write
to your son?
*every week*

**3.** How often do you clean
your windows?
*every month*

**4.** How often do you visit
your aunt in Minnesota?
*every year*

**5.** How often do you wash
your car?
*every weekend*

**6.** How often do your
grandchildren call you?
*every Sunday*

**7.** How often does your boss
say "hello" to you?
*every morning*

**8.** How often do you feed
the animals?
*every afternoon*

**9.** How often do you think
about me?
*all the time*

# She Usually Studies in the Library

| [s] | | [z] | | [ɪz] | | | |
|-----|-----|-----|-----|-----|-----|-----|-----|
| eat | eats | read | reads | wash | washes | always | 100% |
| write | writes | jog | jogs | watch | watches | usually | 90% |
| bark | barks | call | calls | dance | dances | sometimes | 50% |
| speak | speaks | clean | cleans | fix | fixes | rarely | 10% |
| | | | | | | never | 0% |

**A.** Does Carmen usually study in her room?

**B.** No. She rarely studies in her room.
She usually studies in the library.

**1.** Does Linda usually eat lunch in her office?
*rarely*
*in the cafeteria*

**2.** Does Alan always watch the news after dinner?
*never*
*game shows*

**3.** Does Diane sometimes read *The National Star?*
*never*
*Time magazine*

**4.** Does Henry usually wash his car on Sunday?
*rarely*
*on Saturday*

**5.** Does your girlfriend usually jog in the evening?
*sometimes*
*in the afternoon*

**6.** Does your neighbor's dog always bark during the day?
*never*
*at night*

# We Have Noisy Neighbors

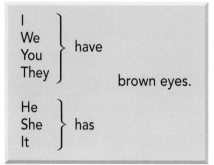

| | |
|---|---|
| I<br>We<br>You<br>They | have |
| | brown eyes. |
| He<br>She<br>It | has |

**A.** Do you have quiet neighbors?

**B.** No. We have noisy neighbors.

---

**1.** Do you have a sister?
*a brother*

**2.** Does this store have an elevator?
*an escalator*

**3.** Does your daughter have straight hair?
*curly hair*

**4.** Does your son have brown hair?
*blond hair*

**5.** Do you and your husband have a dog?
*a cat*

**6.** Does your baby boy have blue eyes?
*brown eyes*

**7.** Do Mr. and Mrs. Hill have a satellite dish?
*an old TV antenna*

**8.** Does your grandmother have a car?
*a motorcycle*

**9.**

My brother and I look very different. I have brown eyes and he has blue eyes. We both have brown hair, but I have short, curly hair and he has long, straight hair. I'm tall and thin. He's short and heavy.

As you can see, I don't look like my brother. We look very different.

**Who in your family do you look like? Who DON'T you look like? Tell about it.**

My sister and I are very different. I'm a teacher. She's a journalist. I live in Miami. She lives in London. I have a large house in the suburbs. She has a small apartment in the city.

I'm married. She's single. I play golf. She plays tennis. I play the piano. She doesn't play a musical instrument. On the weekend I usually watch videos and rarely go out. She never watches videos and always goes to parties.

As you can see, we're very different. But we're sisters . . . and we're friends.

**Compare yourself with a member of your family, another student in your class, or a famous person. Tell how you and this person are different.**

## How to Say It!

### Reacting to Information

**A.** Tell me about *your sister*.
**B.** *She's a journalist. She lives in London.*
**A.** Oh, really? That's interesting.

**Practice conversations with other students. Talk about people you know.**

## CLOSE FRIENDS

My husband and I are very lucky. We have many close friends in this city, and they're all interesting people.

Our friend Greta is an actress. We see her when she isn't making a movie in Hollywood. When we get together with her, she always tells us about her life in Hollywood as a movie star. Greta is a very close friend. We like her very much.

Our friend Dan is a scientist. We see him when he isn't busy in his laboratory. When we get together with him, he always tells us about his new experiments. Dan is a very close friend. We like him very much.

Our friends Bob and Carol are famous television news reporters. We see them when they aren't traveling around the world. When we get together with them, they always tell us about their conversations with presidents and prime ministers. Bob and Carol are very close friends. We like them very much.

Unfortunately, we don't see Greta, Dan, Bob, or Carol very often. In fact, we rarely see them because they're usually so busy. But we think about them all the time.

# ✓ READING CHECK-UP

## WHAT'S THE WORD?

Greta is a famous actress. _____¹ lives in Hollywood. _____² movies are very popular. When _____³ walks down the street, people always say "hello" to _____⁴ and tell _____⁵ how much they like _____⁶ movies.

Dan is always busy. _____⁷ works in _____⁸ laboratory every day. Dan's friends rarely see _____⁹. When they see _____¹⁰, _____¹¹ usually talks about _____¹² experiments. Everybody likes _____¹³ very much. _____¹⁴ is a very nice person.

Bob and Carol are television news reporters. _____¹⁵ friends don't see _____¹⁶ very often because _____¹⁷ travel around the world all the time. Presidents and prime ministers often call _____¹⁸ on the telephone. _____¹⁹ like _____²⁰ work very much.

## LISTENING

**Listen to the conversations. Who and what are they talking about?**

1. a. grandfather
   b. grandmother

2. a. window
   b. windows

3. a. brother
   b. sister

4. a. sink
   b. cars

5. a. neighbor
   b. neighbors

6. a. computer
   b. news reporter

7. a. game show
   b. car

8. a. Ms. Brown
   b. Mr. Wong

9. a. Ken
   b. Jim and Karen

## IN YOUR OWN WORDS

### FOR WRITING AND DISCUSSION

### MY CLOSE FRIENDS

**Tell about your close friends.**

What are their names?
Where do they live?
What do they do?
When do you get together with them?
What do you talk about?

# PRONUNCIATION   Deleted *h*

**Listen.  Then say it.**

I visit her every year.

I write to him every week.

We see her very often.

She calls him every month.

**Say it.  Then listen.**

I visit him every year.

I write to her every week.

We see him very often.

He calls her every month.

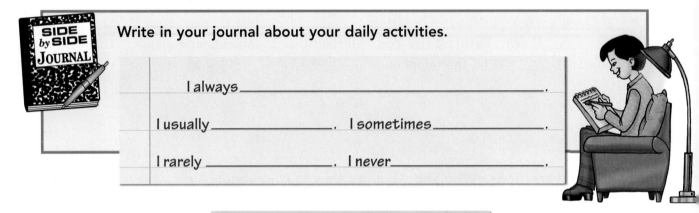

SIDE by SIDE JOURNAL

Write in your journal about your daily activities.

I always _____ .

I usually _____ . I sometimes _____ .

I rarely _____ . I never _____ .

# CHAPTER SUMMARY

## GRAMMAR

### OBJECT PRONOUNS

| He calls | me<br>him<br>her<br>it<br>us<br>you<br>them | every night. |
|---|---|---|

### HAVE/HAS

| I<br>We<br>You<br>They | have | brown eyes. |
|---|---|---|
| He<br>She<br>It | has | |

### SIMPLE PRESENT TENSE: *s* VS. NON-*s* ENDINGS

| He<br>She<br>It | eats.<br>reads.<br>washes. | [s]<br>[z]<br>[ɪz] |
|---|---|---|

| I<br>We<br>You<br>They | eat.<br>read.<br>wash. |
|---|---|

### ADVERBS OF FREQUENCY

| I | always<br>usually<br>sometimes<br>rarely<br>never | wash my car. |
|---|---|---|

## KEY VOCABULARY

### TIME EXPRESSIONS

day        morning
week       afternoon
month      evening
year       night
weekend

### DESCRIBING APPEARANCE

long hair      blond hair      brown eyes
short hair     brown hair      blue eyes
straight hair  black hair
curly hair

# Contrast:
# Simple Present and
# Present Continuous Tenses
# Adjectives

- **Feelings and Emotions**
- **Describing Usual and Unusual Activities**

## VOCABULARY PREVIEW

| | | |
|---|---|---|
| **1.** happy | **5.** hot | **9.** angry |
| **2.** sad | **6.** cold | **10.** nervous |
| **3.** hungry | **7.** tired | **11.** scared |
| **4.** thirsty | **8.** sick | **12.** embarrassed |

# I Always Cry When I'm Sad

cry
crying

**A.** Why are you crying?

**B.** I'm crying because I'm sad.
I ALWAYS cry when I'm sad.

smile
smiling

**A.** Why is she smiling?

**B.** She's smiling because she's happy.
She ALWAYS smiles when she's happy.

shout
shouting

**1. A.** Why are you shouting?

   **B.** _____ angry.

     I ALWAYS _____.

bite
biting

**2. A.** Why is he biting his nails?

   **B.** _____ nervous.

     He ALWAYS _____.

drink
drinking

**3. A.** Why is the bird drinking?

   **B.** _____ thirsty.

     It ALWAYS _____.

shiver
shivering

**4. A.** Why are they shivering?

   **B.** _____ cold.

     They ALWAYS _____.

go
going

**5. A.** Why are they going to
Stanley's Restaurant?

   **B.** _____ hungry.

     They ALWAYS _____.

go
going

**6. A.** Why is she going to
the doctor?

   **B.** _____ sick.

     She ALWAYS _____.

perspire
perspiring

**7. A.** Why are you perspiring?
 **B.** _____ hot.
     I ALWAYS _____ .

blush
blushing

**8. A.** Why is he blushing?
 **B.** _____ embarrassed.
     He ALWAYS _____ .

yawn
yawning

**9. A.** Why is she yawning?
 **B.** _____ tired.
     She ALWAYS _____ .

cover
covering

**10. A.** Why is he covering his eyes?
  **B.** _____ scared.
      He ALWAYS _____ .

## ON YOUR OWN   *What Do You Do When You're Nervous?*

**What do you do when you're nervous?**

When I'm nervous, I perspire.

When I'm nervous, I bite my nails.

When I'm nervous, I walk back and forth.

**Answer these questions.**

What do you do when you're . . .

| | | | | | |
|---|---|---|---|---|---|
| 1. | nervous? | 5. | sick? | 9. | thirsty? |
| 2. | sad? | 6. | cold? | 10. | angry? |
| 3. | happy? | 7. | hot? | 11. | embarrassed? |
| 4. | tired? | 8. | hungry? | 12. | scared? |

**Now ask another student in your class.**

# I'm Washing the Dishes in the Bathtub

**A.** What are you doing?!

**B.** I'm washing the dishes in the bathtub.

**A.** That's strange! Do you USUALLY wash the dishes in the bathtub?

**B.** No. I NEVER wash the dishes in the bathtub, but I'm washing the dishes in the bathtub TODAY.

**A.** Why are you doing THAT?!

**B.** Because my sink is broken.

**A.** I'm sorry to hear that.

**A.** What are you doing?!

**B.** I'm _____.

**A.** That's strange!  Do you USUALLY _____?

**B.** No.  I NEVER _____, but I'm _____ TODAY.

**A.** Why are you doing THAT?!

**B.** Because my _____ is broken.

**A.** I'm sorry to hear that.

**1.** *sleep*
*sleeping* } *on the floor*
*bed*

**2.** *study*
*studying* } *with a*
*flashlight*
*lamp*

**3.** *walk*
*walking* } *to work*
*car*

**4.** *use*
*using* } *a typewriter*
*computer*

**5.** *sweep*
*sweeping* } *the carpet*
*vacuum*

**6.**

## How to Say It!

**Reacting to Bad News**

**A.**  *My sink is broken.*

**B.** { I'm sorry to hear that.
        That's too bad!
        What a shame!

**Practice conversations with other students.
Share some bad news and react to it.**

# READING

## A BAD DAY AT THE OFFICE

Mr. Blaine is the president of the Acme Internet Company. The company has a staff of energetic employees. Unfortunately, all of the employees are out today. Nobody is there. As a result, Mr. Blaine is doing everybody's job, and he's having a VERY bad day at the office!

He's answering the telephone because the receptionist who usually answers it is at the dentist's office. He's typing letters because the secretary who usually types them is at home in bed with the flu. He's sorting the mail because the office assistant who usually sorts it is on vacation. And he's even cleaning the office because the custodian who usually cleans it is on strike.

Poor Mr. Blaine! It's a very busy day at the Acme Internet Company, and nobody is there to help him. He's having a VERY bad day at the office!

 **READING** *CHECK-UP*

### TRUE OR FALSE?

1. Mr. Blaine is the president of the Ajax Internet Company.
2. Mr. Blaine is out today.
3. The secretary is sick.
4. The office assistant is on strike.
5. The custodian isn't cleaning the office today.
6. The receptionist usually answers the phone at the dentist's office.

# LISTENING

**Listen and choose the correct answer.**

1. a. I clean my house.
   b. I'm cleaning my house.
2. a. He sorts the mail.
   b. He's sorting the mail.
3. a. She answers the telephone.
   b. She's answering the telephone.
4. a. Yes. He yawns.
   b. Yes. He's yawning.
5. a. I'm covering my eyes.
   b. I cover my eyes.
6. a. I study in the library.
   b. I'm studying in the library.

# READING

## EARLY MONDAY MORNING IN CENTERVILLE

Early Monday morning is usually a very busy time in Centerville. Men and women usually rush to their jobs. Some people walk to work, some people drive, and others take the bus. Children usually go to school. Some children walk to school, some children take the school bus, and others ride their bicycles. The city is usually very busy. Trucks deliver food to supermarkets, mail carriers deliver mail to homes and businesses, and police officers direct traffic at every corner. Yes, early Monday morning is usually a very busy time in Centerville.

## ✔ READING *CHECK-UP*

**Using the story above as a guide, complete the following:**

### THE SNOWSTORM

Today isn't a typical early Monday morning in Centerville. In fact, it's a very unusual morning. It's snowing very hard there. All the people are at home. The streets are empty, and the city is quiet. The men and women who usually rush to their jobs aren't rushing to their jobs today. The people

who usually walk to work aren't walking, the people who usually drive aren't _____¹, and the people who usually take the bus aren't _____² the bus. The children who usually go to school aren't _____³ to school today. The children who usually walk to school aren't _____⁴ today. The children who usually _____⁵ the school bus aren't _____⁶ it today. And the children who usually _____⁷ their bicycles aren't _____⁸ them this morning.

The city is very quiet. The trucks that usually _____⁹ food aren't _____¹⁰ it today. The mail carriers who usually _____¹¹ mail aren't _____¹² it this morning. And the police officers who usually_____¹³ traffic aren't _____¹⁴ it today. Yes, it's a very unusual Monday morning in Centerville.

# PRONUNCIATION  Reduced *to*

**Listen.  Then say it.**

I'm sorry to hear that.

We go to school.

He listens to the radio.

Mail carriers deliver mail to homes.

**Say it.  Then listen.**

I'm happy to hear that.

They're going to the doctor.

She listens to music.

Trucks deliver food to supermarkets.

Describe a typical day in your city or town.  What do people usually do?  Write about it in your journal.

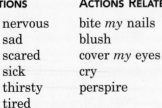

# CHAPTER SUMMARY

## GRAMMAR

### SIMPLE PRESENT TENSE

I always **cry** when I'm sad.

I never **wash** the dishes in the bathtub.

### PRESENT CONTINUOUS TENSE

I'm **crying** because I'm sad.

I'm **washing** the dishes in the bathtub today.

## KEY VOCABULARY

| FEELINGS AND EMOTIONS | | ACTIONS RELATED TO FEELINGS AND EMOTIONS | | EVERYDAY ACTIVITIES | |
|---|---|---|---|---|---|
| angry | nervous | bite *my* nails | shiver | clean | sweep |
| cold | sad | blush | shout | deliver | take the bus |
| embarrassed | scared | cover *my* eyes | smile | drive | type |
| happy | sick | cry | walk back and forth | ride a bicycle | use |
| hot | thirsty | perspire | yawn | sleep | walk |
| hungry | tired | | | study | wash |

## Traffic: A Global Problem

**There are more and more people and more and more cars**

Traffic is a big problem in many cities around the world. Traffic is especially bad during *rush hour*—the time when people go to work or school and the time when they go home. Many people take buses, subways, or trains to work, but many other people drive their cars. As a result, the streets are very busy, and traffic is very bad.

Many cities are trying to solve their traffic problems. Some cities are building more roads. Other cities are expanding their bus and subway systems.

Many cities are trying to reduce the number of cars on their roads. Some highways have *carpool lanes*—special lanes for cars with two, three, or more people. In some cities, people drive their cars only on certain days of the week. For example, in Athens, people with license plate numbers ending in 0 through 4 drive on some days, and people with numbers ending in 5 through 9 drive on other days.

Every day around the world, more and more people drive to and from work in more and more cars. As a result, traffic is a global problem.

## LISTENING

**And Now, Here's Today's News!**

TODAY'S NEWS

| | | |
|---|---|---|
| _b_ | **1** There's a subway problem in . . . | **a.** Toronto |
| ___ | **2** Police officers are on strike in . . . | **b.** Boston |
| ___ | **3** It's snowing very hard in . . . | **c.** Miami |
| ___ | **4** There aren't any problems in . . . | **d.** Sacramento |
| ___ | **5** Children aren't going to school in . . . | **e.** Chicago |

I _____ .

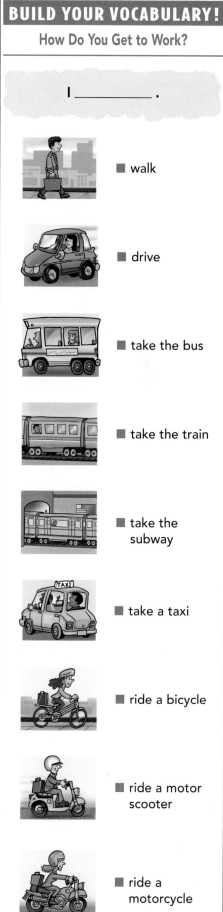

- walk
- drive
- take the bus
- take the train
- take the subway
- take a taxi
- ride a bicycle
- ride a motor scooter
- ride a motorcycle

## Getting Places

**P**eople around the world go to work or school in many different ways.

Some people take the subway.

Some people ride a bicycle.

Some people ride a motor scooter.

Some people even roller-blade!

**How do people go to work or school in different countries you know?**

## FACT FILE

**World's Largest Subway Systems**

| City | Number of Riders in a Year (in millions) | City | Number of Riders in a Year (in millions) |
|------|------|------|------|
| Moscow | 3,160 | Paris | 1,120 |
| Tokyo | 2,740 | Osaka | 1,000 |
| Mexico City | 1,420 | Hong Kong | 779 |
| Seoul | 1,390 | London | 770 |
| New York | 1,130 | Sao Paulo | 701 |

## Global Exchange

**JeffZ:** I live in a small apartment in the center of our city. I have a brother and two sisters. My brother's name is Kevin, and my sisters' names are Emily and Melissa. Our family has a dog and a bird. Our dog's name is Buster, and our bird's name is Lulu. I'm tall, and I have brown eyes. My hair is short and curly. It's usually black, but this week it's red. How about you? Where do you live? Do you have brothers or sisters? What are their names? Do you have a dog or a cat or another pet? What do you look like?

**Send a message to a keypal. Tell about yourself.**

## What Are They Saying?

# Can
# Have to

- **Expressing Ability**
- **Occupations**
- **Looking for a Job**

- **Expressing Obligation**
- **Invitations**

## VOCABULARY PREVIEW

1. actor
2. actress
3. baker
4. chef
5. construction worker
6. dancer
7. mechanic
8. salesperson
9. secretary
10. singer
11. superintendent
12. teacher
13. truck driver

117

# Can You?

Can you speak Hungarian?

No, I can't. But I can speak Romanian.

**1.** Can Betty drive a bus?

**2.** Can Fred cook Italian food?

**3.** Can they ski?

**4.** Can you skate?

**5.** Can Roger use a cash register?

**6.** Can Judy and Donna play baseball?

**7.** Can Rita play the trumpet?

**8.** Can Marvin paint pictures?

Ask another student in your class: "Can you _____?"

# Of Course They Can

**A.** Can Jack fix cars?

**B.** Of course he can.
He fixes cars every day. He's a mechanic.

**1.** Can Michael type?
*secretary*

**2.** Can Barbara teach?
*teacher*

**3.** Can Oscar bake pies and cakes?
*baker*

**4.** Can Jane drive a truck?
*truck driver*

**5.** Can Stanley cook?
*chef*

**6.** Can Claudia sing?
*singer*

**7.** Can Bruce and Helen dance?
*dancers*

**8.** Can Arthur act?
*actor*

**9.** Can Elizabeth and Katherine act?
*actresses*

## THE ACE EMPLOYMENT SERVICE

Many people are sitting in the reception room at the Ace Employment Service. They're all looking for work, and they're hoping they can find jobs today.

Natalie is looking for a job as a secretary. She can type, she can file, and she can use business software on the computer. William is looking for a job as a building superintendent. He can paint walls, he can repair locks, and he can fix stoves and refrigerators.

Sandra is looking for a job as a construction worker. She can use tools, she can operate equipment, and she can build things. Nick is looking for a job as a salesperson. He can talk to customers, he can use a cash register, and he can take inventory. Stephanie and Tiffany are looking for jobs as actresses. They can sing, they can dance, and they can act.

Good luck, everybody! We hope you find the jobs you're looking for!

### Q & A

Natalie, William, Sandra, Nick, Stephanie, and Tiffany are having their interviews at the Ace Employment Service. Using this model, create dialogs based on the story.

**A.** What's your name?
**B.** *Natalie Kramer.*
**A.** Nice to meet you. Tell me, *Natalie,* what kind of job are you looking for?
**B.** I'm looking for a job as *a secretary.*
**A.** Tell me about your skills. What can you do?
**B.** I can *type,* I can *file,* and I can *use business software on the computer.*

## LISTENING

### CAN OR CAN'T?

Listen and choose the word you hear.

1. a. can    b. can't
2. a. can    b. can't
3. a. can    b. can't
4. a. can    b. can't
5. a. can    b. can't
6. a. can    b. can't

### WHAT CAN THEY DO?

Listen and choose what each person can do.

1. a. file    b. type
2. a. cook    b. bake
3. a. repair locks    b. repair stoves
4. a. drive a truck    b. drive a bus
5. a. teach French    b. teach English
6. a. take inventory    b. paint

## ON YOUR OWN *Your Skills*

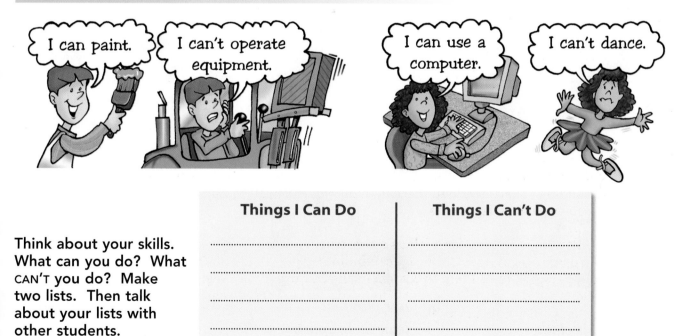

Think about your skills. What can you do? What CAN'T you do? Make two lists. Then talk about your lists with other students.

| Things I Can Do | Things I Can't Do |
|---|---|
| | |
| | |
| | |
| | |

# They Can't Go to Herbert's Party

Herbert is depressed. He's having a party today, but his friends can't go to his party. They're all busy.

A. Can you go to Herbert's party?

B. No, I can't. I have to work.

A. Can Michael go to Herbert's party?

B. No, he can't. He has to go to the doctor.

1. *you and Tom?*
   *fix our car*

2. *Susan?*
   *go to the dentist*

3. *your children?*
   *do their homework*

4. *John?*
   *wash his clothes*

5. *your parents?*
   *clean their apartment*

6. Can YOU go to Herbert's party?

## How to Say It!

### Apologizing

A. Can you *go to a movie* with me on *Saturday*?
B. I'm sorry. I can't. I have to *clean my apartment*.

**Practice the interactions on this page, using "I'm sorry" to apologize.**

## INTERACTIONS

A. Can you _____ with me on _____?
B. I'm sorry. I can't. I have to _____.

**Practice conversations with other students. Practice inviting, apologizing, and giving reasons.**

*go to a soccer game*

*have lunch*

*have dinner*

*go swimming*

*go shopping*

*go dancing*

*go skating*

*go skiing*

*go bowling*

## APPLYING FOR A DRIVER'S LICENSE

Henry is annoyed. He's applying for a driver's license, and he's upset about all the things he has to do.

First, he has to go to the Motor Vehicles Department and pick up an application form. He can't ask for the form on the telephone, and he can't ask for it by mail. He has to go downtown and pick up the form in person.

He has to fill out the form in duplicate. He can't use a pencil. He has to use a pen. He can't use blue ink. He has to use black ink. And he can't write in script. He has to print.

He also has to attach two photographs to the application. They can't be old photographs. They have to be new. They can't be large. They have to be small. And they can't be black and white. They have to be color.

Then he has to submit his application. He has to wait in a long line to pay his application fee. He has to wait in another long line to have an eye examination. And believe it or not, he has to wait in ANOTHER long line to take a written test!

Finally, he has to take a road test. He has to start the car. He has to make a right turn, a left turn, and a U-turn. And he even has to park his car on a crowded city street.

No wonder Henry is annoyed! He's applying for his driver's license, and he can't believe all the things he has to do.

 ✔ **READING** *CHECK-UP*

## WHAT'S THE ANSWER?

1. Can Henry apply for a driver's license on the telephone?
2. Where does he have to go to apply for a license?
3. How does he have to fill out the form?
4. How many photographs does he have to attach to the application?
5. What kind of photographs do they have to be?
6. What does Henry have to do during the road test?

## FIX THIS SIGN!

This sign at the Motor Vehicles Department is wrong. The things people have to do are in the wrong order. On a separate sheet of paper, fix the sign based on the story.

**How to Apply for a Driver's License**

Have an eye examination.
Pay the application fee.
Take a road test.
Pick up an application form.
Take a written test.
Fill out the form in duplicate.

# IN YOUR OWN WORDS

## FOR WRITING AND DISCUSSION

Explain how to apply for one of the following: a passport, a marriage license, a loan, or something else. In your explanation, use "You have to."*

* "You have to" = "A person has to"

# PRONUNCIATION *Can & Can't*

| Listen. Then say it. | Say it. Then listen. |
|---|---|
| I cán type. | We cán dance. |
| She cán teach. | He cán sing. |
| Yes, I can. | Yes, they can. |
| No, he can't. | No, she can't. |

**SIDE** *by* **SIDE JOURNAL**

What do you have to do this week? Write about it in your journal.

## CHAPTER SUMMARY

## GRAMMAR

### CAN

| Can | I he she it we you they | sing? |
|---|---|---|

| I He She It We You They | can | sing. |
|---|---|---|
| | can't | |

| Yes, | I he she it we you they | can. |
|---|---|---|

| No, | I he she it we you they | can't. |
|---|---|---|

### HAVE TO

| I We You They | have to | work. |
|---|---|---|
| He She It | has to | |

## KEY VOCABULARY

### OCCUPATIONS

| | | |
|---|---|---|
| actor | dancer | teacher |
| actress | mechanic | truck driver |
| baker | salesperson | |
| chef | secretary | |
| construction worker | singer | |
| | superintendent | |

### SKILLS

| | | |
|---|---|---|
| act | file | speak *Spanish* |
| bake | fix | take inventory |
| build | operate | talk |
| cook | paint | teach |
| dance | repair | type |
| drive | sing | use |

# Future: Going to
# Time Expressions
# Want to

### 14

- **Describing Future Plans and Intentions**
- **Expressing Wants**
- **Weather Forecasts**
- **Telling Time**
- **Making Predictions**

## VOCABULARY PREVIEW

**Time**

**2:00**
It's two o'clock.

**2:15**
It's two fifteen.
It's a quarter after two.

**2:30**
It's two thirty.
It's half past two.

**2:45**
It's two forty-five.
It's a quarter to three.

**Months of the Year**

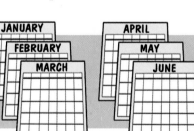
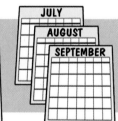

**Seasons**

spring

summer

fall / autumn

winter

# What Are They Going to Do Tomorrow?

| | | |
|---|---|---|
| What | am { I<br>is { he she it<br>are { we you they } | going to do? |

| | | |
|---|---|---|
| (I am)<br>(He is)<br>(She is)<br>(It is)<br>(We are)<br>(You are)<br>(They are) | I'm<br>He's<br>She's<br>It's<br>We're<br>You're<br>They're } | going to read. |

**A.** What's Fred going to do tomorrow?

**B.** He's going to fix his car.

**1.** *Jenny?*

**2.** *Cathy and Dave?*

**3.** *Tony?*

**4.** *you and your brother?*

**5.** *Andrew?*

**6.** *Ashley?*

128

# They're Going to the Beach

| | |
|---|---|
| They're going (to go) to the beach. = | They're going to the beach.<br>They're going to go to the beach. |
| We're going (to go) swimming. = | We're going swimming.<br>We're going to go swimming. |

| today | tomorrow |
|---|---|
| this morning | tomorrow morning |
| this afternoon | tomorrow afternoon |
| this evening | tomorrow evening |
| tonight | tomorrow night |

**A.** What are Mr. and Mrs. Brown going to do tomorrow?

**B.** They're going (to go) to the beach.

1. What's Anita going to do this morning?

2. What are Steve and Brenda going to do tonight?

3. What's Fernando going to do tomorrow evening?

4. What are you and your friends going to do tomorrow afternoon?

**What are YOU going to do tomorrow?**

129

# When Are You Going to . . .?

Time Expressions

this ____
next ____
{
week / month / year
Sunday / Monday / Tuesday / Wednesday / Thursday /
    Friday / Saturday
January / February / March / April / May / June /
    July / August / September / October /
    November / December
spring / summer / fall (autumn) / winter

right now
right away
immediately
at once

130

**Practice conversations with other students. Use any of the time expressions on page 130.**

1. When are you going to clean your garage?

2. When are you going to call your grandmother?

3. When are you going to fix your bicycle?

4. When are you going to visit us?

5. When are you going to wash your car?

6. When are you going to plant flowers this year?

7. When are you going to write to your Aunt Martha?

8. Mr. Smith! When are you going to iron those pants?

**Now ask another student: "When are you going to _____?"**

# READING

## HAPPY NEW YEAR!

It's December thirty-first, New Year's Eve. Ruth and Larry Carter are celebrating the holiday with their children, Nicole and Jonathan. The Carters are a very happy family this New Year's Eve. Next year is going to be a very good year for the entire family.

Next year, Ruth and Larry are going to take a long vacation. They're going to visit Larry's brother in Alaska. Nicole is going to finish high school. She's going to move to San Francisco and begin college. Jonathan is going to get his driver's license. He's going to save a lot of money and buy a used car.

As you can see, the Carters are really looking forward to next year. It's going to be a very happy year for all of them.

Happy New Year!

## ✔ READING CHECK-UP

### COMPUTER CHAT

Fill in the missing words. Then practice this computer chat with another student.

| | |
|---|---|
| **AlexR:** | Jonathan, _____¹ do next year? |
| **JonC:** | _____² get my driver's license. |
| **AlexR:** | And your sister? _____³ do next year? |
| **JonC:** | _____⁴ begin college. |
| **AlexR:** | How about your parents? _____⁵ next year? |
| **JonC:** | _____⁶ take a long vacation. |
| **AlexR:** | Well, Happy New Year, Jonathan! |
| **JonC:** | Happy New Year! |

# LISTENING

Listen and choose the words you hear.

1.  a. Tomorrow.  b. This March.
2.  a. Next December.  b. Next November.
3.  a. Next month.  b. Next Monday.
4.  a. This evening.  b. This morning.
5.  a. This summer.  b. This Sunday.
6.  a. This Tuesday.  b. This Thursday.
7.  a. This afternoon.  b. Tomorrow afternoon.
8.  a. Next year.  b. Next week.
9.  a. Next winter.  b. Next summer.
10.  a. This month.  b. At once.

# What's the Forecast?

| I | | | |
|---|---|---|---|
| We | | want to | |
| You | | | study. |
| They | | | |
| He | | wants to | |
| She | | | |
| It | | | |

**A.** What are you going to do tomorrow?

**B.** I don't know. I want to **go swimming**, but I think the weather is going to be bad.

**A.** Really? What's the forecast?

**B.** The radio says it's going to **rain**.

**A.** That's strange! According to the newspaper, it's going to **be sunny**.

**B.** I hope you're right. I REALLY want to **go swimming**.

1. *have a picnic*
   *rain*
   *be nice*

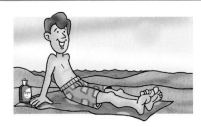

2. *go to the beach*
   *be cloudy*
   *be sunny*

3. *go sailing*
   *be foggy*
   *be clear*

4. *go skiing*
   *be warm*
   *snow*

5. *work in my garden*
   *be very hot*
   *be cool*

6. *take my children to the zoo*
   *be cold*
   *be warm*

**Discuss in class: What's the weather today?**
**What's the weather forecast for tomorrow?**

# What Time Is It?

**2:00**
It's two o'clock.

**2:15**
It's two fifteen.
It's a quarter after two.

**2:30**
It's two thirty.
It's half past two.

**2:45**
It's two forty-five.
It's a quarter to three.

It's noon.
It's twelve noon.

It's midnight.
It's twelve midnight.

**A.** What time does the movie begin?

**B.** It begins at 8:00.

**A.** At 8:00?! Oh no! We're going to be late!

**B.** Why? What time is it?

**A.** It's 7:30! We have to leave RIGHT NOW!

**B.** I can't leave now. I'm SHAVING!

**A.** Please try to hurry! I don't want to be late for the movie.

**A.** What time does _____?

**B.** It _____ at _____.

**A.** At _____?! Oh no! We're going to be late!

**B.** Why? What time is it?

**A.** It's _____! We have to leave RIGHT NOW!

**B.** I can't leave now. I'm _____!

**A.** Please try to hurry! I don't want to be late for the _____.

**1.** What time does the football game begin?
_3:00 / 2:30_
_taking a bath_

**2.** What time does the bus leave?
_7:15 / 6:45_
_packing my suitcase_

**3.** What time does the train leave?
_5:30 / 5:15_
_taking a shower_

**4.** What time does the concert begin?
_8:00 / 7:45_
_looking for my pants_

## How to Say It!

**Asking the Time**

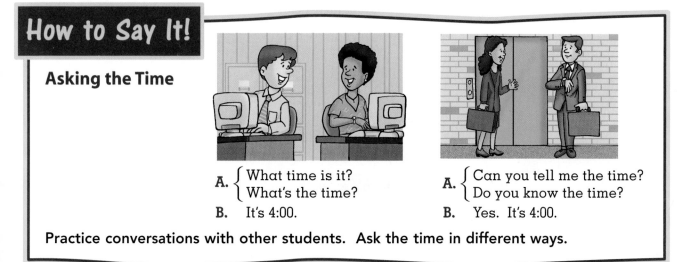

**A.** { What time is it?
      { What's the time?

**B.** It's 4:00.

**A.** { Can you tell me the time?
      { Do you know the time?

**B.** Yes. It's 4:00.

**Practice conversations with other students. Ask the time in different ways.**

## THE FORTUNE TELLER

Walter is visiting Madame Sophia, the famous fortune teller. He's wondering about his future, and Madame Sophia is telling him what is going to happen next year. According to Madame Sophia, next year is going to be a very interesting year in Walter's life.

In January he's going to meet a very nice woman and fall in love.

In February he's going to get married.

In March he's going to take a trip to a warm, sunny place.

In April he's going to have a bad cold.

In May his parents are going to move to a beautiful city in California.

In June there's going to be a fire in his apartment building, and he's going to have to find a new place to live.

In July his friends are going to give him a DVD player for his birthday.

In August his boss is going to fire him.

In September he's going to start a new job with a very big salary.

In October he's going to be in a car accident, but he isn't going to be hurt.

In November he's going to be on a television game show and win a million dollars.

And in December he's going to become a father!

According to Madame Sophia, a lot is going to happen in Walter's life next year. But Walter isn't sure he believes any of this. He doesn't believe in fortunes or fortune tellers. But in January he's going to get a haircut and buy a lot of new clothes, just in case Madame Sophia is right and he meets a wonderful woman and falls in love!

## ✓ READING *CHECK-UP*

### Q & A

**Walter is talking to Madame Sophia. Using these models, create dialogs based on the story.**

**A.** Tell me, what's going to happen in *January*?
**B.** In *January*? Oh! *January* is going to be a very good month!
**A.** Really? What's going to happen?
**B.** *You're going to meet a very nice woman and fall in love.*
**A.** Oh! That's wonderful!

**A.** Tell me, what's going to happen in *April*?
**B.** In *April*? Oh! *April* is going to be a very bad month!
**A.** Really? What's going to happen?
**B.** *You're going to have a bad cold.*
**A.** Oh! That's terrible!

## PRONUNCIATION *Going to & Want to*

> going to = gonna
> want to = wanna

**Listen. Then say it.**

I'm going to study.

It's going to rain.

We want to go swimming.

They want to leave.

**Say it. Then listen.**

He's going to cook.

They're going to paint.

I want to read.

We want to go to the beach.

**SIDE** *by* **SIDE** JOURNAL — What are you going to do tomorrow? Write about it in your journal.

## GRAMMAR

### FUTURE: GOING TO

| | | | |
|---|---|---|---|
| What | am | I | going to do? |
| | is | he<br>she<br>it | |
| | are | we<br>you<br>they | |

| | | |
|---|---|---|
| (I am) | I'm | going to read. |
| (He is) | He's | |
| (She is) | She's | |
| (It is) | It's | |
| (We are) | We're | |
| (You are) | You're | |
| (They are) | They're | |

### TIME EXPRESSIONS

| | | | |
|---|---|---|---|
| I'm going to wash my clothes | today.<br>this morning.<br>this afternoon.<br>this evening.<br>tonight. | tomorrow.<br>tomorrow morning.<br>tomorrow afternoon.<br>tomorrow evening.<br>tomorrow night. | right now.<br>right away.<br>immediately.<br>at once. |

| | | |
|---|---|---|
| I'm going to fix my car | this<br>next | week / month / year.<br>Sunday / Monday / Tuesday / . . . / Saturday.<br>January / February / March / . . . / December.<br>spring / summer / fall (autumn) / winter. |

| | | | |
|---|---|---|---|
| It's | eleven o'clock. | | 11:00 |
| | eleven fifteen. | a quarter after eleven. | 11:15 |
| | eleven thirty. | half past eleven. | 11:30 |
| | eleven forty-five. | a quarter to twelve. | 11:45 |

### WANT TO

| | | |
|---|---|---|
| I<br>We<br>You<br>They | want to | study. |
| He<br>She<br>It | wants to | |

## KEY VOCABULARY

| MONTHS OF THE YEAR | | DAYS OF THE WEEK | SEASONS |
|---|---|---|---|
| January | July | Sunday | spring |
| February | August | Monday | summer |
| March | September | Tuesday | fall / autumn |
| April | October | Wednesday | winter |
| May | November | Thursday | |
| June | December | Friday | |
| | | Saturday | |

# SIDE by SIDE Gazette

**Volume 1**  **Number 6**

# Time Zones

What time is it right now? What time is it in other parts of the world? How do you know?

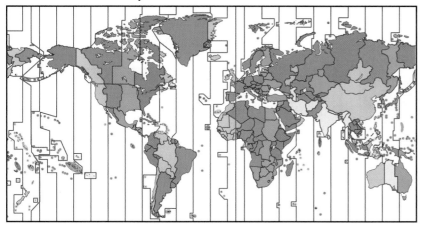

T here are 24 time zones around the world. In each time zone, it is a different hour of the day. The time zone that is east of your time zone is one hour ahead. The time zone to your west is one hour behind. So, for example, when it's 10:00 in Chicago, it's 11:00 in New York, it's 9:00 in Denver, and it's 8:00 in Los Angeles.

New Zealand is 12 time zones to the east of London. Therefore, when it's midnight in London and people are sleeping, it's noon the next day in New Zealand and people are eating lunch!

## FACT FILE

### A Moment in the Life of the World

| TIME AND DAY | PLACE |
|---|---|
| 5:00 A.M.* Monday morning | Los Angeles, USA |
| 7:00 A.M.  Monday morning | Mexico City, Mexico |
| 8:00 A.M.  Monday morning | New York City, USA; Toronto, Canada |
| 9:00 A.M.  Monday morning | Caracas, Venezuela |
| 10:00 A.M.  Monday morning | Rio de Janeiro, Brazil; Buenos Aires, Argentina |
| 1:00 P.M.* Monday afternoon | London, England; Lisbon, Portugal |
| 2:00 P.M.  Monday afternoon | Paris, France; Madrid, Spain; Rome, Italy |
| 3:00 P.M.  Monday afternoon | Athens, Greece; Istanbul, Turkey |
| 4:00 P.M.  Monday afternoon | Moscow, Russia |
| 9:00 P.M.  Monday night | Hong Kong, China |
| 10:00 P.M.  Monday night | Seoul, Korea; Tokyo, Japan |
| 12:00 A.M.  Tuesday morning | Sydney, Australia |

*A.M. = 12:00 midnight to 11:59 in the morning     P.M. = 12:00 noon to 11:59 at night

---

## BUILD YOUR VOCABULARY!

### Occupations

**A. What do you do?**
**B. I'm a / an _____ .**

- ■ architect
- ■ carpenter
- ■ cashier
- ■ farmer
- ■ lawyer
- ■ painter
- ■ pilot
- ■ translator
- ■ waiter
- ■ waitress

## AROUND THE WORLD

### Time and Culture

**P**eople in different cultures think of time in different ways.

In your culture, do people arrive on time for work? Do people arrive on time for appointments? Do people arrive on time for parties? Tell about time in your culture.

## LISTENING

### Thank You for Calling the Multiplex Cinema!

_c_ ①      **a.** *The Fortune Teller*

___ ②      **b.** *Tomorrow Is Right Now*

___ ③      **c.** *The Spanish Dancer*

___ ④      **d.** *The Time Zone Machine*

___ ⑤      **e.** *When Are You Going to Call the Plumber?*

### Global Exchange

**JulieP:** I'm going to be very busy this weekend. On Friday evening, I'm going to get together with my friends from college. We're going to have dinner, and then we're going to a concert. On Saturday morning, I have to clean my apartment because my parents are going to visit me in the afternoon. In the evening, we're going to go bowling. On Sunday I'm going to teach my Sunday school class in the morning, I'm going to a soccer game in the afternoon, and I'm going to wash my clothes in the evening. How about you? What are you going to do this weekend?

Send a message to a keypal. Tell about your plans for the weekend.

### What Are They Saying?

# Past Tense:
# Regular Verbs
# Introduction to Irregular Verbs

- Past Actions and Activities
- Ailments
- Describing an Event
- Making a Doctor's Appointment

## VOCABULARY PREVIEW

1. headache
2. stomachache
3. toothache

4. backache
5. earache
6. cold

7. fever
8. cough
9. sore throat

# How Do You Feel Today?

A. How do you feel today?

B. Not so good.

A. What's the matter?

B. I have a headache.

A. I'm sorry to hear that.

1. stomachache　　2. toothache　　3. backache　　4. earache

5. cold　　6. fever　　7. cough　　8. sore throat

## How to Say It!

**Saying How You Feel**

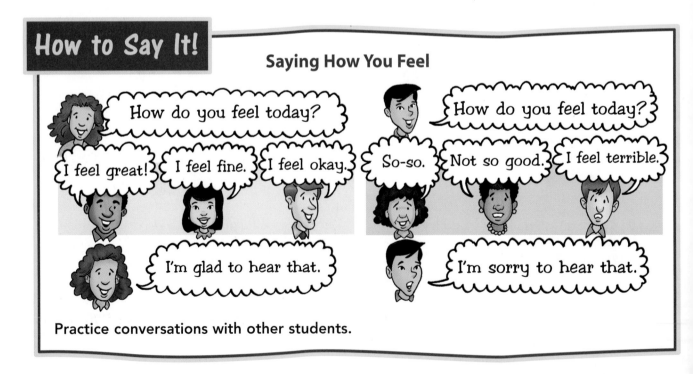

How do you feel today?

I feel great!　I feel fine.　I feel okay.

So-so.　Not so good.　I feel terrible.

How do you feel today?

I'm glad to hear that.

I'm sorry to hear that.

Practice conversations with other students.

# What Did You Do Yesterday?

**{t}**
I work every day.
I work**ed** yesterday.

**{d}**
I play the piano every day.
I play**ed** the piano yesterday.

**{Id}**
I rest every day.
I rest**ed** yesterday.

What did you do yesterday?

I worked.

**{t}**

1. cook
2. wash my car
3. fix my bicycle
4. brush my teeth
5. watch TV
6. type*
7. dance*
8. bake*

**{d}**

9. clean
10. play the piano
11. yawn
12. listen to music
13. shave*
14. smile*
15. cry†
16. study†

**{Id}**

17. shout
18. rest
19. plant flowers
20. wait for the bus

\* type – typed
dance – danced
bake – baked

shave – shaved
smile – smiled

† cry – cried
study – studied

# What's the Matter?

| | |
|---|---|
| I<br>We<br>You<br>They | work every day. |
| He<br>She<br>It | works every day. |

| | |
|---|---|
| I<br>We<br>You<br>They<br>He<br>She<br>It | worked yesterday. |

**A.** How does David feel?

**B.** Not so good.

**A.** What's the matter?

**B.** He has a backache.

**A.** A backache?  How did he get it?

**B.** He played basketball all day.*

\* Or:  all morning / all afternoon / all evening / all night

**1.** *Brian*

**2.** *Linda*

**3.** *you*

**4.** *Gary*

**5.** *Maria*

**6.** *Charlie*

**7.** *Mrs. Clark*

**8.** *you*

**9.** *Carlos*

144

| eat – ate | sing – sang | drink – drank | sit – sat | ride – rode |
|---|---|---|---|---|

**10.** *Daniel*

**11.** *Jennifer*

**12.** *you*

**13.** *Sarah*

**14.** *you*

**15.** *Tim*

## ROLE PLAY *Do You Want to Make an Appointment?*

**You don't feel very well today. Call the doctor's office and make an appointment.**

**A.** Doctor's Office.

**B.** Hello. This is _____.

**A.** Hello, Mr./Ms./Mrs. _____.
How are you?

**B.** Not so good.

**A.** I'm sorry to hear that. What seems to be the problem?

**B.** I _____ all _____ yesterday, and now I have a TERRIBLE _____.

**A.** I see. Do you want to make an appointment?

**B.** Yes, please.

**A.** Can you come in tomorrow at _____ o'clock?

**B.** At _____ o'clock? Yes. That's fine. Thank you.

## THE WILSONS' PARTY

Mr. and Mrs. Wilson invited all their friends and neighbors to a party last night. They stayed home all day yesterday and prepared for the party.

In the morning the Wilsons worked outside. Their daughter, Margaret, cleaned the yard. Their son, Bob, painted the fence. Mrs. Wilson planted flowers in the garden, and Mr. Wilson fixed their broken front steps.

In the afternoon the Wilsons worked inside the house. Margaret washed the floors and vacuumed the living room carpet. Bob dusted the furniture and cleaned the basement. Mr. and Mrs. Wilson stayed in the kitchen all afternoon. He cooked spaghetti for dinner, and she baked apple pies for dessert.

The Wilsons finished all their work at six o'clock. Their house looked beautiful inside and out!

The Wilsons' guests arrived at about 7:30. After they arrived, they all sat in the living room. They ate cheese and crackers, drank lemonade, and talked. Some people talked about their children. Other people talked about the weather. And EVERYBODY talked about how beautiful the Wilsons' house looked inside and out!

The Wilsons served dinner in the dining room at 9:00. Everybody enjoyed the meal very much. They liked Mr. Wilson's spaghetti and they "loved" Mrs. Wilson's apple pie. In fact, everybody asked for seconds.

After dinner everybody sat in the living room again. First, Bob Wilson played the piano and his sister, Margaret, sang. Then, Mr. and Mrs. Wilson showed a video of their trip to Hawaii. After that, they turned on the music and everybody danced.

As you can see, the Wilsons' guests enjoyed the party very much. In fact, nobody wanted to go home!

 **READING** *CHECK-UP*

### WHAT'S THE ANSWER?

1. What did Margaret and Bob Wilson do in the morning?
2. How did Mr. and Mrs. Wilson prepare for the party in the afternoon?
3. When did the guests arrive?
4. Where did the guests sit after they arrived?
5. What did they eat and drink before dinner?
6. What did Margaret do after dinner?
7. What did Mr. and Mrs. Wilson do after dinner?

## LISTENING

**Listen and choose the word you hear.**

| | | |
|---|---|---|
| 1. a. plant | b. planted | |
| 2. a. work | b. worked | |
| 3. a. study | b. studied | |
| 4. a. sit | b. sat | |
| 5. a. drink | b. drank | |
| 6. a. wait | b. waited | |

| | | |
|---|---|---|
| 7. a. finish | b. finished | |
| 8. a. invite | b. invited | |
| 9. a. eat | b. ate | |
| 10. a. clean | b. cleaned | |
| 11. a. wash | b. washed | |
| 12. a. watch | b. watched | |

## IN YOUR OWN WORDS

### FOR WRITING OR DISCUSSION

**A PARTY**

**Tell about a party you enjoyed.**

What did you eat?
What did you drink?
What did people do at the party?
   (eat, dance, talk about . . .)

# PRONUNCIATION  *Past Tense Endings*

**Put these words in the correct column. Then practice saying the words in each column.**

| cleaned | danced | dusted | painted | played | studied | talked | typed | waited |
|---------|--------|--------|---------|--------|---------|--------|-------|--------|

{t}                          {d}                          {ɪd}

_____                    _____                    _____
                             *cleaned*

_____                    _____                    _____

_____                    _____                    _____

**Listen. Then say it.**

I cooked, I cleaned, and I dusted.

I worked, I played, and I planted flowers.

**Say it. Then listen.**

I typed, I studied, and I painted.

I talked, I cried, and I shouted.

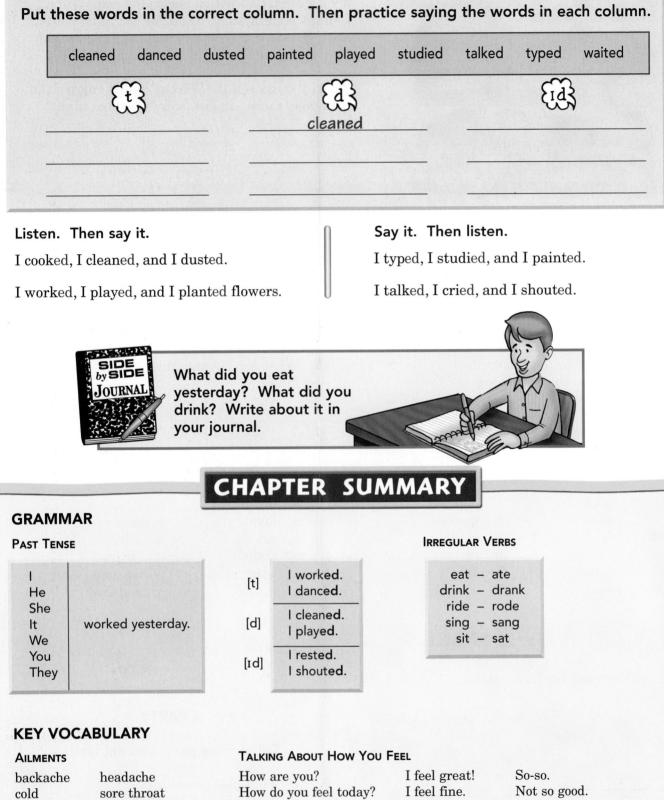

**SIDE by SIDE JOURNAL**

What did you eat yesterday? What did you drink? Write about it in your journal.

## CHAPTER SUMMARY

### GRAMMAR

**PAST TENSE**

| I<br>He<br>She<br>It<br>We<br>You<br>They | worked yesterday. |
|---|---|

| [t] | I worked.<br>I danced. |
|---|---|
| [d] | I cleaned.<br>I played. |
| [ɪd] | I rested.<br>I shouted. |

**IRREGULAR VERBS**

| eat – ate |
|---|
| drink – drank |
| ride – rode |
| sing – sang |
| sit – sat |

### KEY VOCABULARY

**AILMENTS**

| backache | headache |
|---|---|
| cold | sore throat |
| cough | stomachache |
| earache | toothache |
| fever | |

**TALKING ABOUT HOW YOU FEEL**

How are you?
How do you feel today?

What's the matter?

I feel great!
I feel fine.
I feel okay.

So-so.
Not so good.
I feel terrible.

# 16

## Past Tense:
### Yes/No Questions     WH-Questions
### Short Answers     More Irregular Verbs
### Time Expressions

- **Reporting Past Actions and Activities**
- **Giving Reasons**
- **Giving Excuses**

## VOCABULARY PREVIEW

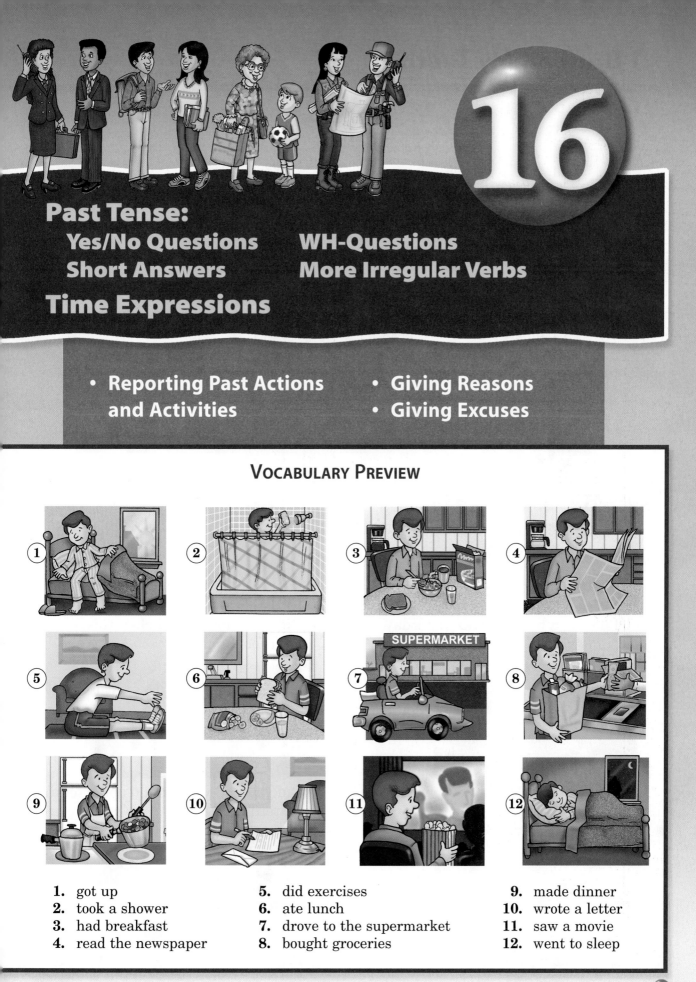

1. got up
2. took a shower
3. had breakfast
4. read the newspaper
5. did exercises
6. ate lunch
7. drove to the supermarket
8. bought groceries
9. made dinner
10. wrote a letter
11. saw a movie
12. went to sleep

# I Brushed My Teeth

I worked.
I didn't work.
  (did not)

Did you work?
  Yes, I did.
  No, I didn't.

| today | yesterday |
| --- | --- |
| this morning | yesterday morning |
| this afternoon | yesterday afternoon |
| this evening | yesterday evening |
| tonight | last night |

Did you brush your hair this morning?

No, I didn't. I brushed my teeth.

**1.** Did he wash his windows yesterday morning?

**2.** Did she paint her kitchen this afternoon?

**3.** Did they study English last night?

**4.** Did you and your friends play tennis yesterday afternoon?

**5.** Did he bake a pie today?

**6.** Did you listen to the news this morning?

# We Went to the Supermarket

I went.
I didn't go.
(did not)

Did you go?
Yes, I did.
No, I didn't.

Did you go to the bank this afternoon?

No, we didn't. We went to the supermarket.

go
went

take
took

1. Did you take the subway this morning?

have
had

2. Did he have a headache last night?

get
got

3. Did Wanda get up at 9:00 this morning?

make
made

4. Did your children make dinner today?

buy
bought

5. Did Michael buy a car yesterday?

do
did

6. Did they do their homework last night?

write
wrote

7. Did Tommy write to his girlfriend this week?

read
read

8. Did you read the newspaper this afternoon?

# TALK ABOUT IT! *What Did They Do Yesterday?*

Yes, { I he she it we you they } did.

No, { I he she it we you they } didn't.

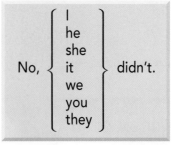

Betty fixed her car yesterday morning.
She washed her windows yesterday afternoon.
She listened to music last night.

Bob read the newspaper yesterday morning.
He went to the library yesterday afternoon.
He wrote letters last night.

Nick and Nancy went to the supermarket
　　yesterday morning.
They bought a new car yesterday afternoon.
They cleaned their apartment last night.

Jennifer did her exercises yesterday
　　morning.
She planted flowers yesterday afternoon.
She took a bath last night.

**Using these models, talk about the people above with other students in your class.**

A. Did *Betty fix her car yesterday morning?*

B. Yes, *she* did.

A. Did *Bob go to the library last night?*

B. No, *he* didn't. *He went to the library yesterday afternoon.*

**How About You?**

What did you do yesterday morning?
What did you do yesterday afternoon?
What did you do last night?

152

**Giving an Excuse**

A. I'm sorry I'm late. *I missed the bus.*

B. I see.

Practice the interactions on this page.
Apologize and give excuses.

## INTERACTIONS

A. I'm sorry I'm late. _____.

B. I see.

I missed the _____.
(bus / train . . .)

I had a _____ this morning.
(headache / stomachache / . . .)

I had to go to the _____.
(doctor / dentist / . . .)

I forgot* my _____ and had to
go back home and get it.
(briefcase / backpack / . . .)

A thief stole* my _____.
(bicycle / car / . . .)

## THINK ABOUT IT! *Good Excuses & Bad Excuses*

The people above have good excuses. Here are some BAD excuses:

I got up late.

I had a big breakfast today.

I met* a friend on the way to work / school.

Discuss with other students: What are some good excuses? What are some bad
excuses? Why are these excuses good or bad?

* forget – forgot    steal – stole    meet – met

153

# READING

## LATE FOR WORK

Victor usually gets up at 7 A.M. He does his morning exercises for twenty minutes, he takes a long shower, he has a big breakfast, and he leaves for work at 8:00. He usually drives his car to work and gets there at 8:30.

This morning, however, he didn't get up at 7 A.M. He got up at 6:30. He didn't do his morning exercises for twenty minutes. He did them for only five minutes. He didn't take a long shower. He took a very quick shower. He didn't have a big breakfast. He had a very small breakfast. He didn't leave for work at 8:00. He left for work at 7:00.

Victor didn't drive his car to work this morning. He drove it to the repair shop. Then he walked a mile to the train station, and he waited for the train for fifteen minutes. After he got off the train, he walked half a mile to his office.

Even though Victor got up early and rushed out of the house this morning, he didn't get to work on time. He got there forty-five minutes late. When his supervisor saw him, she got angry and she shouted at him for five minutes. Poor Victor! He really tried to get to work on time this morning.

## ✔ READING *CHECK-UP*

### WHAT'S THE ANSWER?

1. Did Victor get up at 7 A.M. today?
2. What time did he get up?
3. Did he leave for work at 8:00 this morning?
4. What time did he leave for work?
5. Did he drive his car to the repair shop today?
6. How did he get to the train station?
7. Did Victor get to work on time?
8. Did his supervisor get angry at him?
9. What did she do?

1. Victor ( got up    didn't get up ) at 6:30 A.M. this morning.
2. He ( did    didn't do ) his exercises for twenty minutes today.
3. He ( took    didn't take ) a very quick shower this morning.
4. He ( left    didn't leave ) for work at 8:00 this morning.
5. He ( took    didn't take ) the train to work today.
6. He ( got    didn't get ) to work on time this morning.

## LISTENING

Listen and put a check next to all the things these people did today.

### Carla's Day
___ got up early
___ got up late
___ took a bath
___ took a shower
___ had breakfast
___ had lunch
___ took the subway
___ took the bus
___ met her brother
___ met her mother
___ had dinner
___ made dinner
___ saw a movie
___ saw a play

### Brian's Day
___ fixed his car
___ fixed his bicycle
___ cleaned his garage
___ cleaned his yard
___ painted his bedroom
___ planted flowers
___ washed his windows
___ watched TV
___ read the newspaper
___ read a magazine
___ rode his bicycle
___ wrote to his brother
___ took a shower
___ took a bath

## COMPLETE THE STORY

Complete the story with the correct forms of the verbs.

| buy | eat | get | go | make | see | sit | take |

### SHIRLEY'S DAY OFF

Shirley enjoyed her day off yesterday.  She
_____1 up late, _____2 jogging in the park,
_____3 a long shower, and _____4 a big breakfast.
In the afternoon, she _____5 a movie with her sister.
Then she _____6 groceries at the supermarket, and
she _____7 a big dinner for her parents.  After dinner,
Shirley and her parents _____8 in the living room and
talked.  Shirley had a very nice day off yesterday.

**How About You?**

Tell about a day off YOU enjoyed.  What did you do in the morning? in the afternoon? in the evening?

155

**Listen. Then say it.**

Did you go to the bank?

Did you brush your hair?

Did you listen to the news?

Did you take the subway?

**Say it. Then listen.**

Did you go to the supermarket?

Did you play tennis?

Did you read the newspaper?

Did you see a movie?

 **SIDE by SIDE JOURNAL**

What did you do yesterday? Write in your journal about all the things you did.

# CHAPTER SUMMARY

## GRAMMAR

### PAST TENSE: YES/NO QUESTIONS

| Did | I he she it we you they | work? |
|-----|---|-------|

### SHORT ANSWERS

| Yes, | I he she it we you they | did. |
|------|---|------|

| No, | I he she it we you they | didn't. |
|-----|---|---------|

### PAST TENSE: WH-QUESTIONS

| What did | I he she it we you they | do? |
|----------|---|-----|

### TIME EXPRESSIONS

| Did you study English | yesterday? yesterday morning? yesterday afternoon? yesterday evening? last night? |
|-----------------------|---|

## KEY VOCABULARY

### IRREGULAR VERBS

| | | | | |
|---|---|---|---|---|
| buy – bought | eat – ate | go – went | meet – met | steal – stole |
| do – did | forget – forgot | have – had | read – read | take – took |
| drive – drove | get – got | make – made | see – saw | write – wrote |

# 17

## To Be: Past Tense

- **Television Commercials**
- **Describing Physical States and Emotions**
- **Telling About the Past**
- **Biographies and Autobiographies**

## VOCABULARY PREVIEW

1. sad – happy
2. clean – dirty
3. heavy – thin
4. hungry – full
5. sick – healthy
6. tiny – enormous
7. dull – shiny
8. comfortable – uncomfortable
9. tired – energetic

# PRESTO Commercials

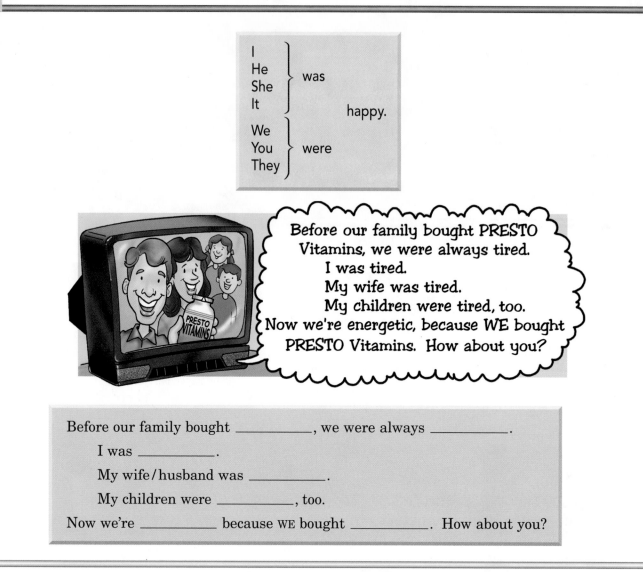

I
He
She
It
⎫ was

We
You
They
⎫ were

happy.

Before our family bought PRESTO
Vitamins, we were always tired.
I was tired.
My wife was tired.
My children were tired, too.
Now we're energetic, because WE bought
PRESTO Vitamins. How about you?

Before our family bought _____, we were always _____.

    I was _____.

    My wife / husband was _____.

    My children were _____, too.

Now we're _____ because WE bought _____. How about you?

**Using the above script, prepare commercials for these other fine PRESTO products.**

1. *sad*        *happy*     2. *hungry*      *full*     3. *dirty*      *clean*

4. *sick*      *healthy*   5. *heavy*     *thin*    6. _____ _____

# Before I Bought PRESTO Shampoo

Before I bought PRESTO Shampoo, my hair **was** always dirty. Now **it's** clean!

1. Before we bought PRESTO Toothpaste, our teeth _____ yellow. Now _____ white!

2. Before we bought PRESTO Paint, our house _____ ugly. Now _____ beautiful!

3. Before I bought a PRESTO armchair, I _____ uncomfortable. Now _____ very comfortable!

4. Before we bought PRESTO Dog Food, our dog _____ tiny. Now _____ enormous!

5. Before I bought PRESTO Window Cleaner, my windows _____ dirty. Now _____ clean!

6. Before we bought PRESTO Floor Wax, our kitchen floor _____ dull. Now _____ shiny!

## How to Say It!

**Recommending Products**

A. Can you recommend a good *toothpaste*?
B. Yes. I recommend *PRESTO Toothpaste*. It's very good.
A. Thanks for the recommendation.

**Practice conversations with other students. Make recommendations about real products.**

# Were You at the Ballgame Last Night?

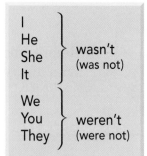

| I He She It | wasn't (was not) |
| We You They | weren't (were not) |

**A.** Were you at the ballgame last night?

**B.** No, I wasn't. I was at the movies.

---

**1.** Was Albert happy yesterday?

**2.** Were they at home this morning?

**3.** Was it cold yesterday?

**4.** Was your grandfather a doctor?

**5.** Was I a quiet baby?

**6.** Were you at home last weekend?

**7.** Was Gloria on time for her plane?

**8.** Were your children late for the school bus?

**9.** Was the food good at the restaurant?

# Did You Sleep Well Last Night?

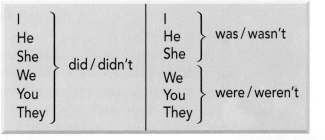

| I He She We You They } did / didn't | I He She } was / wasn't<br>We You They } were / weren't |
|---|---|

**A.** Did you sleep well last night?

**B.** Yes, I did. I was tired.

**A.** Did Roger sleep well last night?

**B.** No, he didn't. He wasn't tired.

---

**1.** Did Frank have a big breakfast today?
*Yes, _____. _____ hungry.*

**2.** Did Thelma have a big breakfast today?
*No, _____. _____ hungry.*

**3.** Did Mr. Chen go to the doctor yesterday?
*Yes, _____. _____ sick.*

**4.** Did Mrs. Chen go to the doctor yesterday?
*No, _____. _____ sick.*

**5.** Did Billy finish his milk?
*Yes, _____. _____ thirsty.*

**6.** Did Katie finish her milk?
*No, _____. _____ thirsty.*

**7.** Did Sonia miss the train?
*Yes, _____. _____ late.*

**8.** Did Stuart miss the train?
*No , _____. _____ late.*

# READING

## MARIA GOMEZ

Maria Gomez was born in Peru. She grew* up in a small village. She began* school when she was six years old. She went to elementary school, but she didn't go to high school. Her family was very poor, and she had to go to work when she was thirteen years old. She worked on an assembly line in a shoe factory.

When Maria was seventeen years old, her family moved to the United States. First they lived in Los Angeles, and then they moved to San Francisco. When Maria arrived in the United States, she wasn't very happy. She missed her friends back in Peru, and she didn't speak one word of English. She began to study English at night, and she worked in a factory during the day.

Maria studied very hard. She learned English, and she got a good job as a secretary. Maria still studies at night, but now she studies advertising at a business school. She wants to work for an advertising company some day and write commercials.

Maria still misses her friends back home, but she communicates with them very often over the Internet. She's very happy now, and she's looking forward to an exciting future.

## ✔ READING *CHECK-UP*

### WHAT'S THE ANSWER?

1. Where was Maria born?
2. Did she grow up in a large city?
3. When did she begin school?
4. What happened when Maria was seventeen years old?
5. Why was Maria unhappy when she arrived in the United States?
6. What is Maria's occupation?
7. What does she want to do in the future?
8. How does Maria communicate with her friends back home?

* grow – grew    begin – began

### WHAT'S THE ORDER?

**Put these sentences in the correct order based on the story.**

____ Maria's family moved to the United States.
____ Maria studies advertising now.
_1_ Maria grew up in a small village.
____ Maria's family moved to San Francisco.
____ Maria worked in a shoe factory.
____ Maria began to study English at night.
____ Maria went to elementary school.
____ Maria's family lived in Los Angeles.
____ Maria got a job as a secretary.

# LISTENING

**Listen and choose the correct answer.**

1. a. They were sick.
   b. They're sick now.
2. a. Their old chairs were comfortable.
   b. Their new chairs are comfortable.
3. a. Lucy was very thirsty.
   b. Lucy wasn't thirsty.
4. a. Fred was on time this morning.
   b. Fred wasn't on time this morning.
5. a. Peter and Mary were at work yesterday.
   b. Peter and Mary are at work today.
6. a. Their kitchen floor wasn't shiny.
   b. Their kitchen floor is dull now.

My Life

# Autobiography

Tell a story about yourself. In your story, answer questions such as:

Where were you born?
Where did you grow up?
Where did you go to school?
What did you study?
When did you move? Where?

# ON YOUR OWN *Do You Remember Your Childhood?*

Yes, { I / he / she / it } was.
{ we / you / they } were.

No, { I / he / she / it } wasn't.
{ we / you / they } weren't.

Yes, { I / he / she / it / we / you / they } did.

No, { I / he / she / it / we / you / they } didn't.

**Answer these questions and then ask other students in your class.**

1. What did you look like?
   Were you tall? thin? pretty? handsome? cute?
   Did you have curly hair? straight hair? long hair?
   Did you have dimples? freckles?

2. Did you have many friends?
   What did you do with your friends?
   What games did you play?

3. Did you like school?
   Who was your favorite teacher? Why?
   What was your favorite subject? Why?

4. What did you do in your spare time?
   Did you have a hobby?
   Did you play sports?

5. Who was your favorite hero?

### Listen. Then say it.

Were you tall?

Did you have long hair?

What did you look like?

Who was your favorite teacher?

### Say it. Then listen.

Were you short?

Did you have freckles?

Where did you grow up?

When did you move?

SIDE by SIDE JOURNAL

Write in your journal about your childhood. What did you look like? What did you do with your friends? Did you like school? What did you do in your spare time?

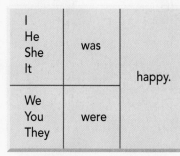

# CHAPTER SUMMARY

## GRAMMAR

### TO BE: PAST TENSE

| I He She It | was | happy. |
| We You They | were | |

| I He She It | wasn't | tired. |
| We You They | weren't | |

| Was | I he she it | late? |
| Were | we you they | |

| Yes, | I he she it | was. |
| | we you they | were. |

| No, | I he she it | wasn't. |
| | we you they | weren't. |

## KEY VOCABULARY

### ADJECTIVES

| | | | | |
|---|---|---|---|---|
| beautiful | enormous | heavy | shiny | ugly |
| clean | exciting | hungry | sick | uncomfortable |
| comfortable | full | late | thin | |
| dirty | good | poor | thirsty | |
| dull | happy | quiet | tiny | |
| energetic | healthy | sad | tired | |

### VERBS RELATED TO LIFE EVENTS

| | |
|---|---|
| arrive | live |
| be born | move |
| begin – began | study |
| grow up – grew up | work |

# Advertisements

## How do advertisers sell their products?

Advertisements are everywhere! They are on television, on the radio, and in newspapers and magazines. Ads are also on billboards, on buses and trains, and even in movie theaters. People get advertisements in their mail. There are also a lot of advertisements on the Internet.

Advertisements are sometimes in unusual places—in elevators, on top of taxis, and in public bathrooms. People sometimes carry signs with ads on the street, and small airplanes sometimes carry signs in the sky. Advertisers are always looking for new places for their ads.

## FACT FILE

| Countries Where Advertisers Spend the Most Money | | |
|---|---|---|
| United States | Brazil |
| Japan | Italy |
| United Kingdom | Australia |
| Germany | Canada |
| France | Korea |

## LISTENING

### And Now a Word From Our Sponsors!

| | | | | |
|---|---|---|---|---|
| _d_ | ① | Dazzle | a. | floor wax |
| ___ | ② | Shiny-Time | b. | dog shampoo |
| ___ | ③ | Energy Plus | c. | throat lozenges |
| ___ | ④ | Lucky Lemon Drops | d. | toothpaste |
| ___ | ⑤ | K-9 Shine | e. | vitamins |

## BUILD YOUR VOCABULARY!

### Opposites

- dark
- light
- fancy
- plain
- fast
- slow
- good
- bad
- heavy
- light
- high
- low
- long
- short
- neat
- messy
- open
- closed
- wet
- dry

## Shopping

**P**eople around the world buy things in different ways.

This person is shopping in a store.

These people are buying things at an outdoor market.

This person is ordering something from a catalog over the telephone.

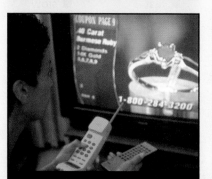

This person is buying something from a home shopping channel on TV.

These people are looking for things at a yard sale.

This person is shopping on the Internet.

**What are the ways people buy things in different countries you know?**

### Global Exchange

TedG: I had a very busy day today. I got up at 6:30, took a shower, ate breakfast, and went to school. In my English class this morning, I read a long story, and I wrote my autobiography. I didn't have time for lunch because I had to meet with my Spanish teacher. After I met with her, I went to math class. We had a big test today. It was very difficult! After school, I went to a basketball game. Then I went home, did some homework, had dinner, and did some more homework. How about you? What did you do today?

Send a message to a keypal. Tell about what you did today.

### What Are They Saying?

# Listening Scripts

## Chapter 1 – Page 5

*Listen and choose the correct answer.*

1. A. What's your name?
   B. Mary Black.
2. A. What's your address?
   B. Two sixty-five Main Street.
3. A. What's your apartment number?
   B. Five C.
4. A. What's your telephone number?
   B. Two five nine – four oh eight seven.
5. A. What's your social security number?
   B. Oh three two – eight nine – six one seven nine.
6. A. What's your e-mail address?
   B. maryb-at-worldnet-dot-com.

## Chapter 2 – Page 15

### WHAT'S THE WORD?

*Listen and choose the correct answer.*

1. Mr. and Mrs. Lee are in the park.
2. Jim is in the hospital.
3. She's in the living room.
4. He's in the kitchen.
5. They're in the basement.
6. We're in the yard.

### WHERE ARE THEY?

*Listen and choose the correct place.*

1. A. Where's David?
   B. He's in the living room.
2. A. Where's Patty?
   B. She's in the bedroom.
3. A. Where are Mr. and Mrs. Kim?
   B. They're in the yard.
4. A. Where are you?
   B. I'm in the bathroom.
5. A. Where's the telephone book?
   B. It's in the kitchen.
6. A. Where are you and John?
   B. We're in the basement.

## Chapter 3 – Page 23

*Listen and choose the correct answer.*

1. What are you doing?
2. What's Mr. Carter doing?
3. What's Ms. Miller doing?
4. What are Jim and Jane doing?
5. What are you and Peter doing?
6. What am I doing?

## *Side by Side* Gazette – Page 26

*Listen to the messages on Bob's machine. Match the messages.*

You have seven messages.

Message Number One: "Hello. I'm calling for Robert White. This is Henry Drake. Mr. White, please call me at 427-9168. That's 427-9168. Thank you." [*beep*]

Message Number Two: "Hi, Bob! It's Patty. How are you? Call me!" [*beep*]

Message Number Three: "Bob? Hi. This is Kevin Carter from your guitar class. My phone number is 298-4577." [*beep*]

Message Number Four: "Mr. White? This is Linda Lee, from the social security office. Please call me. My telephone number is 969-0159." [*beep*]

Message Number Five: "Hello, Bob? This is Jim. I'm in the park. We're playing baseball. Call me, okay? My cell phone number is 682-4630." [*beep*]

Message Number Six: "Hello. Mr. White? This is Mrs. Lane on River Street. Your dog is in my yard. Call me at 731-0248." [*beep*]

Message Number Seven: "Hello, Bob. This is Dad. I'm at home. I'm reading the newspaper. Mom is planting flowers in the yard. It's a beautiful day. Where are you? What are you doing? Call us." [*beep*]

## Chapter 4 – Page 33

*Listen and choose the correct answer.*

1. What are you eating?
2. What is she reading?
3. What is he playing?
4. What are they painting?
5. What are you watching?
6. What is he washing?

## Chapter 5 – Page 43

### WHAT'S THE ANSWER?

*Listen and choose the correct answer.*

1. Tell me about your apartment.
2. Tell me about your new car.
3. Tell me about your neighbors.
4. How's the weather?
5. Tell me about your hotel.
6. How's the food at the restaurant?

### TRUE OR FALSE?

*Listen to the conversation. Then answer True or False.*

A. Hello.
B. Hello. Is this Betty?
A. Yes, it is.
B. Hi, Betty. This is Louise. I'm calling from Mud Beach.
A. From Mud Beach?
B. Yes. I'm on vacation in Mud Beach for a few days.
A. How's the weather in Mud Beach?
B. It's terrible! It's cold, and it's cloudy.
A. Cold and cloudy? What a shame! How's the hotel?
B. The hotel is terrible! It's old, it's noisy, and the rooms are very small.
A. I'm sorry to hear that. Tell me about the restaurants.
B. The restaurants in Mud Beach are expensive, and the food isn't very good. In fact, I'm having problems with my stomach.
A. What a shame! So, Louise, what are you doing?
B. I'm sitting in my room, and I'm watching TV. I'm not having a very good time.
A. I'm sorry to hear that.

## Chapter 6 – Page 51

### QUIET OR NOISY?

*Listen to the sentence. Are the people quiet or noisy?*

1. He's listening to loud music.
2. She's reading.
3. He's sleeping.
4. The band is playing.
5. Everybody is singing and dancing.
6. He's studying.

### WHAT DO YOU HEAR?

*Listen to the sound. What do you hear? Choose the correct answer.*

1. [Sound: singing]
2. [Sound: crying]

3. [Sound: vacuuming]
4. [Sound: laughing]
5. [Sound: drums]

*Side by Side* Gazette – Page 54

*Listen to the weather reports. Match the weather and the cities.*

This is Robby T. with the weather report from WXBC. It's a hot day in Honolulu today. The temperature here is one hundred degrees, and everybody is swimming at the beach.

This is Annie Lu with the weather report from WCLD in Atlanta. It's snowing here in Atlanta today, and everybody is at home.

This is Herbie Ross with today's weather from KFTG radio. It's warm and sunny here in Los Angeles today. The temperature is seventy degrees. It's a beautiful day.

This is Jimmy G. with your weather on CHME radio. It's cool and sunny here in Toronto today. It's a very nice day.

This is Lisa Lee with your WQRZ weather report. It's cold and cloudy in Chicago today. The temperature here is thirty-two degrees. Yes, it's a cold and cloudy day!

## Chapter 7 – Page 65

### WHAT PLACES DO YOU HEAR?

*Listen and choose the correct places.*

Ex.: My neighborhood is very nice. There's a supermarket across the street, and there's a video store around the corner.

1. My neighborhood is very convenient. There's a bank around the corner and a laundromat across the street.
2. My neighborhood is very noisy. There's a fire station next to my building, and there's a gas station across the street.
3. The sidewalks in my neighborhood are very busy. There's a school across the street and a department store around the corner.
4. There are many small stores in the center of my town. There's a bakery, a drug store, and a book store.
5. My neighborhood is very busy. There's a hotel across the street, and the hotel is between a hospital and a health club.

### TRUE OR FALSE?

*Listen to the conversation. Then answer True or False.*

A. Tell me about the apartment.
B. There's a large living room, a large kitchen, a nice bathroom, and a very nice bedroom.
A. How many closets are there in the apartment?
B. There's a closet in the bedroom and a closet in the living room.
A. Oh, I see. And how many windows are there in the living room?
B. There are four windows in the living room.
A. Four windows?
B. Yes. That's right.
A. Tell me. Is there a superintendent in the building?
B. Yes, there is.
A. And are there washing machines in the basement?
B. Yes, there are. There are three washing machines.
A. Oh, good. Tell me, is there an elevator in the building?
B. No, there isn't. But there's a fire escape.

## Chapter 8 – Page 75

### WHAT'S THE WORD?

*Listen and choose the correct answer.*

1. A. May I help you?
   B. Yes, please. I'm looking for a blouse.

2. A. Can I help you?
   B. Yes, please. I'm looking for a pair of boots.
3. A. May I help you?
   B. Yes, please. I'm looking for a necklace.
4. A. Can I help you?
   B. Yes, please. I'm looking for a raincoat.
5. A. May I help you?
   B. Yes, please. I'm looking for a pair of stockings.
6. A. Can I help you?
   B. Yes, please. I'm looking for a shirt.

### WHICH WORD DO YOU HEAR?

*Listen and choose the correct answer.*

1. These jackets are expensive.
2. I'm looking for a leather belt.
3. I'm wearing my new wool sweater.
4. Suits are over there.
5. Is this your shoe?
6. Polka dot ties are very popular this year.

*Side by Side* Gazette – Page 77

*Listen to these announcements in a clothing store. Match the clothing and the aisles.*

Attention, J-Mart Shoppers! Are you looking for a black leather jacket? Black leather jackets are very popular this year! There are a lot of black leather jackets at J-Mart today! They're in Aisle 9, next to the coats.

Attention, J-Mart Shoppers! Are you looking for a pair of vinyl gloves? Vinyl gloves are very popular this year! Well, there are a lot of vinyl gloves at J-Mart today! They're in Aisle 5, across from the hats.

Attention, J-Mart Shoppers! Are you looking for a blouse? Is red your favorite color? Red blouses are very popular this year! There are a lot of red blouses at J-Mart today. They're in Aisle 7, next to the dresses.

Attention, J-Mart Shoppers! Are you looking for a special gift for your mother, your wife, or your sister? A silver bracelet is a special gift for that special person. All our silver bracelets are in Aisle 1, across from the earrings.

Attention, J-Mart Shoppers! Are you looking for a special gift for your father, your husband, or your brother? A polka dot tie is a special gift for that special person. All our polka dot ties are in Aisle 11, next to the belts.

## Chapter 9 – Page 84

*Listen and choose the correct answer.*

1. My brother lives in Chicago.
2. My name is Peter. I work in an office.
3. This is my friend Carla. She speaks Italian.
4. My sister drives a bus in Chicago.
5. We read the newspaper every day.
6. My parents visit their friends every weekend.
7. Charlie cooks in a Greek restaurant.
8. My brother and I paint houses.
9. My friend Betty calls me every day.
10. My parents usually shop at the mall.

## Chapter 10 – Page 93

### WHAT'S THE WORD?

*Listen and choose the word you hear.*

1. Do you work on Monday?
2. Does your daughter go to this school?
3. We do a different activity every Sunday.
4. Larry doesn't play a sport.
5. We don't go to Stanley's Restaurant.
6. Sally goes to a health club every week.
7. She baby-sits for her neighbors every Thursday.
8. They go to work every morning.

*Listen and choose the correct response.*

1. Do you speak Korean?
2. Does Mrs. Wilson go to Stanley's Restaurant?
3. Does your sister live in Los Angeles?
4. Do you and your brother clean the house together?
5. Does your husband like American food?
6. Do you go to school on the weekend?
7. Do you and your friends play tennis?
8. Does your cousin live in this neighborhood?

*Side by Side* Gazette – Page 98

*You're calling the International Cafe! Listen to the recorded announcement. Match the day of the week and the kind of entertainment.*

Hello! This is the International Cafe—your special place for wonderful entertainment every day of the week! Every day the International Cafe presents a different kind of entertainment. On Monday, Antonio Bello plays Italian classical music. On Tuesday, Miguel Garcia reads Spanish poetry. On Wednesday, Amanda Silva sings Brazilian jazz. On Thursday, Nina Markova reads Russian short stories. On Friday, Hiroshi Tanaka plays Japanese rock music. On Saturday, Rita Rivera sings Mexican popular music. And on Sunday, Slim Wilkins sings American country music. So come to the International Cafe—your special place for wonderful entertainment . . . every day of the week!

## Chapter 11 – Page 105

*Listen to the conversations. Who and what are they talking about?*

1. A. How often do you visit him?
   B. I visit him every week.
2. A. How often do you wash them?
   B. I wash them every year.
3. A. Do you write to her very often?
   B. I write to her every month.
4. A. Is it broken?
   B. Yes. I'm fixing it now.
5. A. How often do you see them?
   B. I see them every day.
6. A. How often do you use it?
   B. I use it all the time.
7. A. When does he wash it?
   B. He washes it every Sunday.
8. A. Do you see him very often?
   B. No. I rarely see him.
9. A. Do you study with them very often?
   B. Yes. I study with them all the time.

## Chapter 12 – Page 112

*Listen and choose the correct answer.*

1. What are you doing?
2. What does the office assistant do?
3. What's the receptionist doing?
4. Is he tired?
5. What do you do when you're scared?
6. Where do you usually study?

*Side by Side* Gazette – Page 115

*Listen to these news reports. Match the news and the city.*

A. You're listening to WBOS in Boston. And now here's Randy Ryan with today's news.
B. Good morning. Well, the people in Boston who usually take the subway to work aren't taking it today. There's a big problem with the subway system in Boston.

A. You're listening to KSAC in Sacramento. And now here's Jessica Chen with the morning news.

B. Good morning. The big news here in Sacramento is the traffic! Sacramento police officers are on strike today, and nobody is directing traffic. There are traffic problems all around the city!

A. This is WCHI in Chicago. And now here's Mike Maxwell with today's news.
B. Good morning. It's snowing very hard in Chicago right now. As a result, the streets of the city are empty. People aren't walking or driving to work. There aren't any trucks or buses on the street. And mail carriers aren't delivering the mail.

A. You're listening to CTOR in Toronto. And now here's Mark Mitchell with today's news.
B. It's a quiet Tuesday morning in Toronto. There aren't any bad traffic problems right now, and there aren't any problems with the subway system or the buses.

A. You're listening to WMIA in Miami. And now here's today's news.
B. Good morning. This is Rita Rodriguez with the news. The children of Miami who usually take school buses to school aren't taking them this morning. The men and women who drive the school buses are on strike. Some children are walking to school today. Many students are staying home.

## Chapter 13 – Page 121

*Listen and choose the word you hear.*

1. I can speak Spanish.
2. He can't paint.
3. She can type.
4. We can't build things.
5. They can use tools.
6. We can't operate equipment.

*Listen and choose what each person can do.*

1. He can't file. He can type.
2. They can cook. They can't bake.
3. She can repair locks. She can't repair stoves.
4. I can't drive a truck. I can drive a bus.
5. He can teach French. He can't teach English.
6. We can take inventory. We can't paint.

## Chapter 14 – Page 132

*Listen and choose the words you hear.*

1. A. When are you going to buy a computer?
   B. Tomorrow.
2. A. When are your neighbors going to move?
   B. Next November.
3. A. When are you going to visit me?
   B. Next month.
4. A. When are you going to do your laundry?
   B. This evening.
5. A. When are you going to begin your vacation?
   B. This Sunday.
6. A. When are we going to go to the concert?
   B. This Thursday.
7. A. When are you going to wash the windows?
   B. This afternoon.
8. A. When is she going to get her driver's license?
   B. Next week.
9. A. When is your daughter going to finish college?
   B. Next winter.
10. A. When is the landlord going to fix the kitchen sink?
    B. At once.

*Listen and match the theaters and the movies.*

Thank you for calling the Multiplex Cinema! The Multiplex Cinema has five theaters with the best movies in town!

Now showing in Theater One: *The Spanish Dancer,* a film from Spain about the life of the famous dancer Carlos Montero. Show times are at one fifteen, three thirty, and seven o'clock.

Now showing in Theater Two: *When Are You Going to Call the Plumber?*, starring Julie Richards and Harry Grant. In this comedy, a husband and wife have a lot of problems in their new house. Show times are at two thirty, four forty-five, and seven fifteen.

Now showing in Theater Three: *The Fortune Teller*. In this film from Brazil, a woman tells people all the things that are going to happen in their lives. Show times are at five o'clock, seven forty-five, and ten fifteen.

Now showing in Theater Four: *The Time Zone Machine*, the exciting new science fiction movie. Professor Stanley Carrington's new machine can send people to different time zones around the world. Show times are at five fifteen, eight o'clock, and ten thirty. There's also a special show at midnight.

Now showing in Theater Five: *Tomorrow Is Right Now*. In this new drama, a truck driver from Australia falls in love with a businesswoman from Paris. Where are they going to live, and what are they going to tell their friends? See it and find out! Show times are at six o'clock, eight thirty, and ten forty-five.

The Multiplex Cinema is on Harrison Avenue, across from the shopping mall. So come and see a movie at the Multiplex Cinema. You're going to have a good time! Thank you, and have a nice day!

## Chapter 15 – Page 147

*Listen and choose the word you hear.*

1. We plant flowers in our garden in the spring.
2. I worked at the office all day.
3. They studied English all morning.
4. Mr. and Mrs. Jones sit in their living room all day.
5. They drank lemonade all summer.
6. I waited for the bus all morning.
7. They finish their work at five o'clock.
8. We invited our friends to the party.
9. I eat cheese and crackers.
10. She cleaned her apartment all afternoon.
11. We wash our clothes at the laundromat.
12. He watched TV all evening.

## Chapter 16 – Page 155

*Listen and put a check next to all the things these people did today.*

Carla got up early this morning. She took a shower, she had breakfast, and she took the subway to work. She didn't have lunch today. She left work at five thirty, and she met her mother at six o'clock. They had dinner at a restaurant. Then they saw a movie.

Brian had a busy day today. This morning he fixed his car. Then he cleaned his yard. This afternoon he planted flowers, and then he washed his windows. This evening he read the newspaper, and he wrote to his brother. Then he took a bath.

## Chapter 17 – Page 163

*Listen and choose the correct answer.*

1. Before we bought Captain Crispy Cereal, we were always sick. Now we're always healthy.
2. We bought new chairs for our living room because our old chairs were very uncomfortable. We love our new chairs. They're VERY comfortable.

3. My daughter Lucy didn't finish her milk this morning. She wasn't very thirsty.
4. Fred was very upset this morning. He was late for the bus, and he didn't get to work on time.
5. Hmm. Where are Peter and Mary? They were at work yesterday, but they aren't here today.
6. Our kitchen floor was very dull. Our neighbors recommended Sparkle Floor Wax, and now our kitchen floor isn't dull any more. It's shiny!

*Listen and match the products.*

ANNOUNCER: And now a word from our sponsors.
WOMAN: I had a problem with my teeth. They were very yellow, and I was upset. I went to my dentist, and she recommended Dazzle. So I went to the store and I bought some. Now I brush my teeth with Dazzle every day. My teeth aren't yellow any more. They're white. They're VERY white! Thank you, Dazzle!
ANNOUNCER: Are YOUR teeth yellow? Try Dazzle today!

TED: Bob! This kitchen floor is beautiful!
BOB: Thanks, Ted.
TED: Is it new?
BOB: Oh, no! This is my old kitchen floor.
TED: But it's so shiny!
BOB: That's right, Ted. It IS shiny, because I bought Shiny-Time!
TED: Shiny-Time?
BOB: Yes. Shiny-Time!
ANNOUNCER: That's right, Ted. YOU can have a shiny kitchen floor, too. Use Shiny-Time . . . every time!

WOMAN: Alan? What's the matter?
MAN: I don't know. I jog all the time, but today I'm really tired. Tell me, Julie, you're NEVER tired. You're always energetic. How do you do it?
WOMAN: Energy Plus!
MAN: Energy Plus?
WOMAN: Yes, Alan, Energy Plus! Before I bought Energy Plus, I was always tired like you. But now I'm energetic all the time!
ANNOUNCER: Tired? Try Energy Plus today! You can find it in supermarkets and drug stores everywhere.

PRESIDENT: Thank you. Thank you very much.
ASSISTANT: That was excellent, Mr. President.
PRESIDENT: Thank you, Ron. You know, I have a terrible sore throat.
ASSISTANT: I can hear that, Mr. President. Here. Try one of these.
PRESIDENT: What are they?
ASSISTANT: Lucky Lemon Drops.
PRESIDENT: Lucky Lemon Drops?
ASSISTANT: Yes, Mr. President. They're really good for a sore throat.
PRESIDENT: Thanks, Ron.
ANNOUNCER: Lucky Lemon Drops. They're good for the president! They're good for you!

WOMAN: My dog's fur was dull. It was VERY dull, and my dog was very sad. Then I bought K-9 Shine! Yes, K-9 Shine. I washed my dog with K-9 Shine, and now his fur is shiny! It's very shiny, and my dog is very happy!
ANNOUNCER: Try K-9 Shine today! YOUR dog's fur can be shiny, too!

# Thematic Glossary

## Ailments 141

backache
cold
cough
earache
fever
headache
sore throat
stomachache
toothache

## Classroom Objects

board 8
book 7
bookshelf 8
bulletin board 8
chair 8
clock 8
computer 7
desk 7
dictionary 8
globe 8
map 8
notebook 8
pen 7
pencil 7
ruler 8
table 8
wall 8

## Clothing

bathrobe 77
belt 67
blouse 67
boot 68
bracelet 68
briefcase 68
coat 67
dress 67
earring 68
glasses 68
glove 68
hat 68
jacket 67
jeans 67
mitten 68
necklace 68
pajamas 67
pants 67
pocketbook 68
purse 68
raincoat 75
ring 77
sandals 77
scarf 77
shirt 67
shoe 67
shorts 77
skirt 67
slippers 77
sneakers 77
sock 67
sports jacket 72
stocking 68
suit 67
sunglasses 73
sweat pants 77
sweater 67
tee shirt 77
tie 67
umbrella 68

wallet 77
watch 68

## Colors 70

black
blue
brown
gold
gray
green
orange
pink
purple
red
silver
white
yellow

## Days of the Week 87

Sunday
Monday
Tuesday
Wednesday
Thursday
Friday
Saturday

## Describing Feelings and Emotions

angry 49
annoyed 124
cold 40
depressed 122
embarrassed 107
happy 22
hot 40
hungry 107
nervous 107
sad 77
scared 107
sick 107
thirsty 107
tired 49

## Describing People and Things

active 90
athletic 90
bad 112
beautiful 22
big 35
blond 102
busy 29
cheap 35
clean 72
closed 165
comfortable 157
cute 163
dark 165
difficult 35
dirty 72
dry 165
dull 157
easy 35
empty 72
energetic 112
enormous 157
exciting 162
expensive 35

fancy 165
fast 165
fat 35
frustrated 75
full 157
good 42
handsome 35
happy 22
healthy 157
heavy 35
high 165
inexpensive 75
interesting 13
large 35
late 161
light 165
little 35
long 165
loud 35
low 165
married 35
messy 165
neat 165
new 35
noisy 35
old 35
open 165
outgoing 94
plain 165
poor 35
popular 94
pretty 35
quiet 35
rich 35
sad 77
shiny 157
short 35
shy 94
single 35
slow 165
small 35
tall 35
thin 35
tiny 157
ugly 35
uncomfortable 157
wet 165
young 35

## Everyday Activities

act 48
baby-sit 87
bake 47
brush *their* teeth 27
call 79
clean 27
comb *my* hair 97
cook 17
cry 47
dance 48
deliver 113
do *our* exercises 30
do *their* homework 28
do *yoga* 87
drink 17
drive 79
eat 17
feed 27
fix 27
get dressed 97
get up 97

go 89
go *dancing* 87
go to bed 97
go to school 97
go to work 97
have *dinner* 46
jog 87
laugh 50
listen to 17
paint 27
plant 17
play *baseball* 17
play *cards* 17
play the *piano* 17
read 17
ride 46
see 87
sell 79
shave 135
shop 63
sing 17
skate 118
skateboard 47
ski 118
sleep 17
speak 79
study 17
sweep 111
swim 17
take a bath 97
take a shower 97
take a taxi 115
take the bus 113
take the subway 115
take the train 115
talk 50
teach 17
type 112
use 53
vacuum 49
visit 79
walk 111
wash 27
watch TV 17
work 79
write 42

## Family Members

aunt 45
brother 45
brother-in-law 54
children 45
cousin 45
daughter 45
daughter-in-law 54
father 45
father-in-law 54
grandchildren 45
granddaughter 45
grandfather 45
grandmother 45
grandparents 45
grandson 45
husband 45
mother 45
mother-in-law 54
nephew 45
niece 45
parents 45
sister 45
sister-in-law 54
son 45
son-in-law 54
uncle 45
wife 45

## Months of the Year 127

January
February
March
April
May
June
July
August
September
October
November
December

## Occupations

actor 3
actress 3
architect 139
baker 117
carpenter 139
cashier 139
chef 117
construction worker 117
custodian 112
dancer 117
farmer 139
journalist 103
lawyer 139
mail carrier 113
mechanic 117
office assistant 112
painter 139
pilot 139
police officer 113
receptionist 112
salesperson 117
secretary 117
singer 117
superintendent 59
teacher 15
translator 139
truck driver 117
waiter 139
waitress 139

## Personal Information

address 1
apartment number 4
e-mail address 4
fax number 4
first name 4
last name 4
name 1
phone number 1
telephone number 1

## Places Around Town

airport 63
bakery 55
bank 7
barber shop 55
book store 55
bus station 55
cafeteria 21
church 21
clinic 37
clothing store 63
department store 55
drug store 55
factory 162
fire station 56
gas station 56

hair salon 55
health club 31
hospital 14
hotel 42
laundromat 31
library 7
movie theater 14
park 14
police station 57
post office 7
restaurant 7
school 55
shopping mall 63
supermarket 7
train station 55
video store 55
zoo 14

## Places at Home

attic 10
basement 10
bathroom 7
bedroom 7
dining room 7
garage 10
kitchen 7
living room 7
yard 10

## Seasons 127

spring
summer
fall/autumn
winter

## Skills

act 48
bake 47
build 115
cook 17
dance 48
file 120
fix 27
operate 120
paint 27
repair 120
sing 17
sort the *mail* 112
speak *Spanish* 79
take inventory 120
talk 50
teach 17
type 112
use 111

## Time Expressions

afternoon 92
day 22
evening 92
month 99
morning 92
night 49
week 92
weekend 83
year 70

## Weather 40

cloudy
cold
cool
hot
rain
snow
sunny
warm

## Cardinal Numbers

| | | | |
|---|---|---|---|
| 1 | one | 20 | twenty |
| 2 | two | 21 | twenty-one |
| 3 | three | 22 | twenty-two |
| 4 | four | . | . |
| 5 | five | . | . |
| 6 | six | 29 | twenty-nine |
| 7 | seven | 30 | thirty |
| 8 | eight | 40 | forty |
| 9 | nine | 50 | fifty |
| 10 | ten | 60 | sixty |
| 11 | eleven | 70 | seventy |
| 12 | twelve | 80 | eighty |
| 13 | thirteen | 90 | ninety |
| 14 | fourteen | 100 | one hundred |
| 15 | fifteen | 200 | two hundred |
| 16 | sixteen | . | . |
| 17 | seventeen | . | . |
| 18 | eighteen | 900 | nine hundred |
| 19 | nineteen | 1,000 | one thousand |
| | | 2,000 | two thousand |
| | | . | . |
| | | 10,000 | ten thousand |
| | | 100,000 | one hundred thousand |
| | | 1,000,000 | one million |

## Irregular Verbs: Past Tense

| | |
|---|---|
| be | was |
| begin | began |
| buy | bought |
| do | did |
| drink | drank |
| drive | drove |
| eat | ate |
| forget | forgot |
| get | got |
| go | went |
| grow | grew |
| have | had |
| make | made |
| meet | met |
| read | read |
| ride | rode |
| see | saw |
| sing | sang |
| sit | sat |
| steal | stole |
| take | took |
| write | wrote |

# Index